THE MOMENT ADAM SINNED IN HIS GARDEN—AND ALL MEN DIED

ADAM'S BROTHER LEFT HIS GARDEN (GETHSEMANE), DIED ON A CROSS AND ALL MEN LIVED

ROMANS 5:12–21 UNVEILED AND REVEALED

Jim Taylor

NHP

Taylor/New Harbor Press
1601 Mt. Rushmore Rd, Ste 3288
Rapid City, SD 57701
www.newharborpress.com

The Moment Adam Sinned in His Garden—And All Men Died Adam's Brother Left His Garden (Gethsemane), Died on a Cross—And All Men LIved/Jim Taylor —1st ed.
ISBN 978-1-63357-296-6

To Judy, a beautiful and wonderful wife of many years

From a loving husband

Jim has written five other books.

JESUS

The Perfect Man in Whom Dwells the Fullness of God

LEVITICUS, UNVEILED AND REVEALED

The Lamb and the Altar, the Lamb of God and the Cross

REVELATION TO JOHN'S APOCALYPSE UNVEILED AND
REVEALED

The Spiritual View of a Carnal War

HEBREWS UNVEILED AND REVEALED

Leviticus Fulfilled by the Coming of Jesus

I AM

I AM Jehovah, Lord of Israel—*I AM* Jesus, Lord of
Christians

Contents

ABOUT THIS BOOK

WHEN PAUL WROTE HIS letter to the Romans, he authored a book that is very important, because it offers hope to the lost— but part of his letter is not so easy to understand, and even the apostle Peter recognized that (2 Peter 3:14-16). There is a passage of Scripture in Paul's letter (Romans 5:12-21) that is very difficult to grasp—not because it is difficult to read and understand, the words Paul used mean exactly what they say—it is difficult to comprehend because of the message it contains. It proclaims that when Adam sinned his one act of disobedience condemned the creation, made all men sinners, and sentenced all men to death; and for that reason many of the brethren, and most churches, do not accept those Scriptures for what they say— because they just don't sound like something the Almighty God who is good, holy, just, righteous, and love—would do. But the catholic church accepts them, and that is why its leadership—the Pope—demands that little babies must be baptized immediately after they are born, or they will perish for Adam's transgression. For babies to have to be taken to a priest and sprinkled with a little water when they are born, or else they will perish, is not reasonable. Little babies have no sin, they are not head accountable for Adam's transgression, and they never have been—all because of the cross. Also, not one little baby should ever have to depend on someone else to do something for them that would save their souls, something over which they have no control whatsoever. The only One we all must depend on to save our souls is Jesus.

By considering only the first part of each verse of Romans 5:12-19, that view sums up the message of doom that was caused by Adam's trespass: "Therefore, as through one man sin entered into the world, and death through sin; and so death passed unto all men, for that all sinned" (v12); "For if by the trespass of the one the many died" (v15); "for the judgment came of one unto condemnation" (v16); "For if, by the trespass of the one, death reigned through the one" (v17); "So then as through one trespass the judgment came unto all men to condemnation" (v18); "For as through the one man's disobedience the many were made sinners" (v19). From this it is very clear that it was just one trespass, and only one trespass, or Adam's sin, that condemned the creation and caused the reign of death.

When we view the second part of those verses in like manner, we see the summation of the power of Jesus and his cross that annulled Adam's trespass and canceled its consequences. They declare: "much more did the grace of God, and the gift by the grace of the one man, Jesus Christ, abound unto the many" (v15); "but the free gift came of many trespasses unto justification." (V16); "much more shall they that receive the abundance of grace and of the gift of righteousness reign in life through the one, even Jesus Christ" (v17); "even so through one act of righteousness the free gift came unto all men to justification of life" (v18); "even so through the obedience of the one shall the many be made righteous" (v19).

Why is it so difficult to put those verses together as a unit, just as they are written, and accept them for what they say? Doing that declares that just as it was one act of disobedience that condemned the creation and sentenced all men to death, so also it was just one act of righteous obedience—the life and the cross of Jesus—that immediately annulled Adam's sin, restored the creation back to its original perfection, set all men free from sin and death—and gave them eternal life—if they will accept it. Jesus summed all of this up very well when he said to Martha, "I am the resurrection, and the life: he that believeth on me, though he die, yet shall he live; and whosoever liveth and believeth on me shall never die. Believest thou this?" (John 11:25–26).

The problem is: the catholic church leadership recognizes only the first part of the verses of Romans 5:15-19 and failing to accept the second part they acknowledge only the condemnation Adam's sin caused. That is so sad! It is the last part of each of those verses that declares the righteous act of Jesus (dying on a cross) that *immediately* canceled Adam's transgression and annulled its consequences the moment it happened.

This book agrees with the catholic church's view that the day Adam sinned God did in fact threaten to condemn the entire creation and sentence all men to death—for that is the message of Romans 5:12–21. Further along in Paul's letter to the Romans, Paul declared that what God threatened to do did happen: "For the creation was subjected to vanity, not of its own will, but by reason of him who subjected it, in hope that the creation itself also shall be delivered from the bondage of corruption into the liberty of the glory of the children of God. For we know that the whole creation groaneth and travaileth in pain together until now" (Romans 8:20-22). "And inasmuch as it is appointed unto men once to die, and after this cometh judgment" (Hebrews 9:27). All of that transpired the day Adam sinned.

But this book is also in agreement with the conservative Christian churches' view that God would never hold little children and innocent people accountable for the sin of another man, which is also the message of Romans 5:12–21. Not only are both views of Romans 5:12–21 possible, but they are the only views conceivable. Adam's one act of disobedience condemned

3

the creation, Jesus' one act of righteousness (the cross) saved it, and the free gift of eternal life that was established by the cross makes both views correct. How can that be possible? It was made possible because of the cross.

When Adam sinned, the death sentence that God declared against all men because of his trespass was immediately nailed to the cross of Jesus, and it was there that one Man instantly paid in full for all the devastation his brother's sin had caused. Adam and Jesus were brothers because they both had the same Father. The first son of God, Adam (Luke 3:38), committed a trespass that condemned everything his Father made. The second Son of God, the only begotten Son of God who is called Jesus (Matthew 16:13-17; Hebrews 4:14) died on a cross to pay in full for the devastation his brother's trespass had caused. Therefore, the death sentence that was declared against the creation and the entire human family was immediately taken away, nullified, and nailed to the cross of Jesus the very moment the trespass was committed; and not for one instant was any man or child held accountable for what Adam had done. The purpose of this book is to explain all of that in simple language that can be easily understood, and not make something out of it that is not there.

But how could all men be set free from the consequences of Adam's transgression the moment he sinned when it required the cross of Jesus and his resurrection to accomplish that? Jesus did not die on the cross until about 33 A.D. Adam sinned in the very beginning of time. The answer: it is because the cross and all its power to forgive sinners and bestow eternal life was an established fact in the mind of God before the foundation of the world. God knew that Adam would sin and condemn the creation, and he was prepared to correct that problem the moment it happened. Peter wrote:

> And if ye call on him as Father, who without respect of persons judgeth according to each

man's work, pass the time of your sojourning in fear: knowing that ye were redeemed, not with corruptible things, with silver or gold, from your vain manner of life handed down from your fathers; but with precious blood, as of a lamb without spot, even the blood of Christ: who was foreknown indeed before the foundation of the world, but was manifested at the end of the times for your sake, who through him are believers in God, that raised him from the dead, and gave him glory; so that your faith and hope might be in God. (1 Peter 1:17-21)

Therefore, the power of the cross and all its benefits were already in place the moment Adam sinned, and so his trespass was immediately annulled the very instant it happened. The price, or the "ransom" (Matthew 20:28; 1 Timothy 2:6) that God paid to accomplish that is so valuable, and so precious, that it is far beyond description. That is just the way God does things. That is why not one little baby or any other person—*that is, except Jesus*—were ever held accountable and forced to face death for Adam's trespass. But without Jesus and his cross, and his resurrection—it would all have been an entirely different story (1 Corinthians 15:12-20).

Adam and Eve were God's children. They were created in the image of God (Genesis 1:26–27), and God was their only Father. They had no mother. They had been given everything God owned except for one small object—a tree—and that tree belonged to God. It was called the Tree of Knowledge of Good and Evil. Adam and Eve were forbidden to eat of the fruit of that tree upon the pain of death, and that was the only law they were given to obey; if they did not break that one law there was no other way they could have sinned. Moses wrote, "And Jehovah God commanded the man, saying, Of every tree of the garden thou mayest freely eat: but of the tree of the knowledge of good and evil, thou shalt not eat of it: for in the day that thou eatest thereof thou shalt surely die" (Genesis 2:16–17).

That tree had a purpose: It offered a continual way for Adam and Eve to prove their respect and their love for their Father by staying away from his tree. But Adam and Eve were not pleased with all that God had given them—they wanted more. They saw no reason for God to prevent them from having that tree as well as all the other trees, and so they ate the forbidden fruit, and sinned. The devastation, the pain, the misery, and the grief they caused by their one act of rebellion is far beyond description. Adam and Eve were sentenced to death the very day they rebelled against God when they ate of the fruit of his tree. That day they suffered spiritual death by being driven away from the presence of God and forced out of their beautiful garden (Genesis 3:22–24). They also suffered physical death because that day their bodies started to grow old and decline. It was some 930 years later that Adam experienced physical death (Genesis 5:5). We do not know what happened to Adam and Eve after they left the garden. They were both offered forgiveness for having sinned against the Almighty. The fact that Adam lived for 930 years after he sinned proves that (Romans 2:4; 2 Peter 3:9, 15)—for he was not immediately destroyed because of his sin—he was given time to repent. The serpent was condemned instantly for its sin because for it there was no hope of it being restored to its former glory.

So, what happened? Why would Adam's trespass, which appears to be just a simple act of disobedience cause the creation to have all the problems it has? It was because of Adam's trespass that the world in which we live today is not the same world God created. The world God made in the beginning was perfect, glorious, and without blemish. There were no such things as diseases, illness, hunger, thirst, poverty, pain, suffering, or aging—And there was no sin, and there was no death. There were no destroying forces caused by terrible storms and other natural catastrophes that just destroyed everything in their path. All the horrible disasters that still occur in our world today are the leftover consequences of Adam's transgression. They shall be abolished when Jesus comes again, the dead are raised, and the new heavens and the new earth are established. When that transpires it will complete the restoration of all things (Acts 3:21; 2 Peter 3:1–13).

Before Adam sinned the world was in perfect harmony with itself and with the Creator, and all the earth was at peace. There was no violence because at that time Adam and Eve and the entire animal world were all vegetarians—they ate nothing but fruits and vegetables (Genesis 1:29–30). That did not change until after the flood (Genesis 9:1-4). Therefore, nothing had to die so an animal would become food for something larger, stronger, or smarter than they were. That made life for Adam and Eve quite comfortable and very simple. All they had to do every day was "to dress and to keep" the garden which gave them something to do (Genesis 2:15) —and pick and eat the fruit from the trees as they worked. They were also to have children and replenish the earth with their own kind (Genesis 1:28). That would give them plenty to do. They were to enjoy the garden and each other in their marriage relationship. Every day they would walk and talk with their Father who had given them the garden, and who had given them life. They had a perfect world to live in, a perfect life to live, and a perfect fellowship with God, their Father (Genesis 3:8–9). What more could they ask for?

With Adam's trespass that all changed. The world in which we live is subject to many threatening things—earthquakes, volcanic eruptions, terrible hurricanes, tornedos, storms, famines, plagues, fires, floods, pestilence, wars, crime, poverty, pain, disappointments—and even the violence of evil men who love to rob, kill, and destroy. All those things came into the world by the trespass of just one man.

It is impossible for us to even imagine how God felt the day that happened, for God did not just lose his children; he lost his entire human family and his whole creation. Adam and Eve stood condemned because of their disobedience, and the entire world that God made and had given them was condemned with them (Romans 8:18–23); because they, and the entire creation in which they lived were all one united entity. Therefore, when any part of it became defiled, it all became corrupt, and the only correction for such a disaster was the complete annihilation of everything God had made. If ever we should feel sorry for God, and maybe even pray for God, it should be because of that day, for that was the day when God's world just completely fell apart. God has the same feelings and emotions we have, because he is the one who has given us ours (Genesis 6:5-13).

PREFACE

THERE ARE PASSAGES OF Scripture in the Bible that are quite complex, and therefore they are difficult to comprehend. One such example is the book of Daniel, especially chapter 11. The revelation letter that John wrote to the Seven Churches of Asia is an example of Bible Scriptures that are not easy to grasp. When the Scriptures prophesy of things that are yet to come, and the writer of those Scriptures used figurative sayings and complex expressions to make their point, those Scriptures can be difficult to comprehend.

However, there are other parts of the Bible that are difficult to understand for other reasons—not because they contain a complex message, but because they speak of things that are in direct conflict with what a person already believes to be the established truth. Therefore, those Scriptures can be difficult to accept for exactly what they say because of prejudice. When that occurs it is a great temptation to force those Scriptures into agreement with flawed perspectives. We do not like to think we have been wrong in the teachings that we have been steeped in for all our lives.

Romans 5:12–21 is an example of that dilemma because there are two messages in those ten verses of Scripture, and most people see only one message. One of the messages (the one that most people solely acknowledge) is the threat of despair unto death that was caused by Adam's trespass. That is the message which is in the first part of each verse, and it is the only message the catholic church acknowledges. The other message is the power of the free gift—the forgiveness of sin and the promise of eternal life (Romans 6:23). It is the free gift that annuls the consequence of Adam's trespass and immediately restores life to those who had been threatened with condemnation and death because of Adam's trespass. That message of hope and encouragement appears in the second part of each verse of those Scriptures.

Adam's sin was his act of rebellion and disobedience in breaking God' law; the free gift (eternal life) was established by the faithfulness and obedience of Jesus, Adam's brother, when he gave himself up to be crucified to take away the sins of the world (John 1:29). Therefore, those two messages are diametrically opposed to each other—they are exact opposites. Paul wrote, "But not as the trespass, so also is the free gift. For if by the trespass of the one the many died, much more did the grace of God, and the gift by the grace of the one man, Jesus Christ, abound unto the many" (Romans 5:15). Therefore, when a person reads the first part of the verses of Scripture in Romans 5:12–21, they are viewing the condemnation and the devastation that Adam's sin caused. When a person reads the second part of those scriptures, they see the power of the cross that immediately canceled Adam's sin, annulled its consequences, set all men free from sin and death, and took away all the sins of the world (John 1:29). The free gift that was established by Jesus' obedience in going to the cross is just as prevalent as is the message of doom and despair that was caused by Adam's disobedience when he ate the forbidden fruit—but the message of hope, joy, peace, and the salvation that Jesus offers to all men by his free gift is much more powerful. It is that message of hope and joy in Romans 5:12–21 that is the *"much more"* that many brethren fail to see. All that most people see when they read Romans 5:12–21 is the message of doom and despair, and that is so very sad.

Romans 5:12–21 is the passage of Scripture the catholic church uses to teach (correctly) that Adam condemned himself, the whole creation, and the entire human race when he sinned. But that is also the same passage of scripture that the catholic church uses to require little babies to be baptized (sprinkled with water by a priest), and that is not correct. I believe the catholic Church's view to be correct as far as teaching that God threatened to condemn the entire creation because of Adam's transgression, but the teaching that little babies must be sprinkled with water when they are born, or they will perish, is not reasonable. It is far from the truth. Little babies have no sin, they have not sinned, and they are not held accountable for the trespass that Adam committed (Matthew 18:2–6). If that doctrine were true little babies would be lost through no fault of their own—they would perish because someone failed to take them to a priest and have them sprinkled with water.

The condemnation that God pronounced against the world because of Adam's trespass never actually fell upon the human family, and it certainly did not fall upon little babies—Because it immediately fell upon one Man: Jesus. Adam's sin was immediately nailed to the cross of Jesus and annulled the very moment it was committed. Therefore, not one person, and that certainly includes little babies, have ever been held accountable for Adam's trespass, nor shall any person ever be held accountable for what Adam did—*except Jesus.* Jesus took the full responsibility and all of the guilt for Adam's trespass upon himself, and he paid in full for all the devastation and corruption Adam's sin caused with the blood of his cross. Therefore, all men shall be held accountable to God, but only for their own sins—the sins that they themselves commit when they reach the age of accountability. In the

Old Testament the age of accountability was twenty years of age (Numbers 14:28–32).

The conservative churches, such as the Churches of Christ and other Christian churches believe (correctly) that Adam's sin never condemned little babies or anyone else in the human population. The reason they believe that is: it would be totally contrary for the righteous Almighty God to hold a little child or an innocent person accountable for the trespass of another man. Therefore, their view of Romans 5:12–21 is that babies do not have to be baptized until they grow up and they are held accountable for their own sins, the sins they themselves had committed, which is the true and correct view, but it is true only because of the cross. If there had been no cross, and no resurrection, then all men—and that includes little babies—would have been forever held captive in the bondage of sin and death because of Adam's trespass. If there had been no cross there could be no resurrection, and without the resurrection there is no hope of life after death for anyone, and that includes little children. Proof of that statement is as follows in Paul's letter the Corinthians:

> Now if Christ is preached that he hath been raised from the dead, how say some among you that there is no resurrection of the dead? But if there is no resurrection of the dead, neither hath Christ been raised: and if Christ hath not been raised, then is our preaching vain, your faith also is vain. Yea, and we are found false witnesses of God; because we witnessed of God that he raised up Christ: whom he raised not up, if so be that the dead are not raised. For if the dead are not raised, neither hath Christ been raised: and if Christ hath not been raised, your faith is vain; ye are yet in your sins. Then they also that are fallen asleep in Christ have perished. If we have only hoped in

Christ in this life, we are of all men most pitiable. But now hath Christ been raised from the dead, the firstfruits of them that are asleep.

Behold, I tell you a mystery: We all shall not sleep, but we shall all be changed, in a moment, in the twinkling of an eye, at the last trump: for the trumpet shall sound, and the dead shall be raised incorruptible, and we shall be changed. For this corruptible must put on incorruption, and this mortal must put on immortality. But when this corruptible shall have put on incorruption, and this mortal shall have put on immortality, then shall come to pass the saying that is written, Death is swallowed up in victory. O death, where is thy victory? O death, where is thy sting? The sting of death is sin; and the power of sin is the law: but thanks be to God, who giveth us the victory through our Lord Jesus Christ. (1 Corinthians 15:12-20, 51–57)

It was the cross of Jesus and his resurrection from the tomb that conquered death and gave all men their victory over sin and death—and that victory is assured to all who believe that Jesus is the Christ, the Son of God, and He was raised from the tomb by his resurrection (Romans 10:9). It was the very moment that Jesus was raised from the grave that the victory over death became an established fact, and sin died. Jesus became sin for us, and when Jesus was nailed to the cross and died, it was sin that was nailed to the cross and perished. Paul wrote, "Him who knew no sin he made to be sin on our behalf; that we might become the righteousness of God in him" (2 Corinthians 5:21).

The above is a clear and sensible view of Romans 5:12–21, and it gives a sound reason that explains how Adam's trespass condemned the whole creation; but it also explains how Jesus immediately took that curse upon himself and paid for it in full by his death on the cross, and his resurrection. It is Jesus' cross and resurrection that freed the creation from the bondage of sin, which is death. Romans 5:12–21 has a serious message, but that message is not difficult to understand, it says what it means, and it means what it says—But for many it is very difficult to accept. Here it is, Romans 5:12–21:

> Therefore, as through one man sin entered into the world, and death through sin; and so death passed unto all men, for that all sinned: —for until the law sin was in the world; but sin is not imputed when there is no law. Nevertheless death reigned from Adam until Moses, even over them that had not sinned after the likeness of Adam's transgression, who is a figure of him that was to come. But not as the trespass, so also is the free gift. For if by the trespass of the one the many died, much more did the grace of God, and the gift by the grace of the one man, Jesus Christ, abound unto the many. And not as through one that sinned, so is the gift: for the judgment came of one unto condemnation, but the free gift came of many trespasses unto justification. For if, by the trespass of the one, death reigned through the one; much more shall they that receive the abundance of grace and of the gift of righteousness reign in life through the one, even Jesus Christ. So then as through one trespass the judgment came unto all men to condemnation; even so through one act of righteousness the free gift came unto all men to justification of life. For as through the one man's disobedience the many were made sinners, even so through the obedience of the one

shall the many be made righteous. And the law came in besides, that the trespass might abound; but where sin abounded, grace did abound more exceedingly: that, as sin reigned in death, even so might grace reign through righteousness unto eternal life through Jesus Christ our Lord.

The reason Romans 5:12–21 is so difficult to comprehend is not because of the way it is written, or because of the words Paul used to put it all together. It is difficult to comprehend because it says something that is very challenging to believe: that God would declare the judgment of death against innocent people, and even little babies, for the trespass that one man committed. But that is exactly what the first part of the verses in Romans 5:12–21 says God did, and this book will illustrate why he did it. It was because God is holy, righteous, and just, and he cannot tolerate sin nor anything that sin has contaminated—and it was Adam's trespass that corrupted the whole creation and condemned the entire human family. Therefore, God paid the supreme price himself to do away with all sin and take away the sins of the world (John 1:29). The price God paid was the death of his own Son on a cruel cross. It was Jesus who suffered the death sentence for Adam's trespass the very moment Adam sinned, because the cross was in the mind of God before the foundation of the world (1 Peter 1:17–21).

The plan God had to create the world was in his mind from the beginning (Revelation 4:11), and His plan to redeem the creation from sin and death was part of that plan. That is why not one person had to suffer the consequence of Adam's trespass themselves (death): because Jesus paid for it in full with his own blood (Acts 20:28). That is what established the righteousness of God when he declared condemnation and death against all men for the sin of one man, but He never allowed that judgment to fall upon the human family—It is because it all fell upon another man, and just one Man in the human family: His name is Jesus, and that Man was himself the Almighty Jehovah God.

When we read Romans 5:12–21 we encounter five statements that express the contrast between Adam, his trespass, and its deadly effect: —contrasted against Christ, his holy and righteous act of obedience, and how it established the grace of God and eternal life for all men. In those verses of Scripture we should look for three things: *the trespass, the free gift, and "much more,"* The trespass was Adam's original sin. The free gift is the power of the cross to annul Adam's trespass and establish the forgiveness of sin and the free gift of eternal life. Romans 6:23 says, "For the wages of sin is death; but the free gift of God is eternal life in Christ Jesus our Lord." The *"much more"* is what separates the message of condemnation unto death that was caused by Adam's trespass (as it is affirmed in the first part of each verse), from the message of how the free gift of Christ has the power to completely annul the consequence of Adam's trespass (as it is asserted in the last part of each verse). By viewing those verses of Scripture in that way we can understand the devastating effect Adam's trespass had on God's world and on the entire human family. We can also see how the free gift of Christ had the power to annul Adam's sin by paying in full the price that was demanded to restore God's creation back into its original perfection, glory, and beauty. It was the cross of Jesus that immediately restored life to all who had been judged and condemned because of Adam's sin. Likewise, it is the free gift that offers the forgiveness of sin and eternal life to all who had died because of their own sins (the sins that they themselves have committed). For the free gift that takes away the sins that a person commits himself (not Adam's trespass, but their own sins), belief in the Christ to be the Son of God and obedience to God's Word is absolutely necessary (John 8:24; John 8:31–32).

There is a Scripture that sums up Romans 5:12–21 perfectly. It is 1 Corinthians 15:21–22 which says, "For since by man came death, by man came also the resurrection of the dead. For as in Adam all die, so also in Christ shall all be made alive." There is another Scripture in Romans 5 that says about the same thing:

So then as through one trespass the judgment came unto all men to condemnation; even so through one act of righteousness the free gift came unto all men to justification of life. For as through the one man's disobedience the many were made sinners, even so through the obedience of the one shall the many be made righteous. (Romans 5:18–19)

Those Scriptures say that when Adam sinned it was he, and he alone, who condemned the entire creation by his one act of disobedience. All other men—including those who had not yet been born—were helpless to do anything to escape the consequence of Adam's trespass, and therefore they stood condemned by his sin. They were going to be born into a condemned world and they would be condemned with it. However, when Jesus died on the cross, he annulled Adam's transgression and saved all men from its consequences, and that includes babies who had not yet been born. Jesus achieved all of that alone by his sinless life and his death on the cross.

Without their participation or knowledge all living creatures were condemned by Adam's trespass; and without their participation or knowledge all living creatures were freed from the consequence of Adam's trespass—because Jesus immediately took that condemnation upon himself and paid for it in full with his cross. It was one man's unrighteous act of disobedience that threatened all men with death and made them all sinners. It was another Man's righteous act of obedience that annulled Adam's sin, set all men free from its consequences, and gave them eternal life—and made them all righteous. It was the power of the cross that accomplished all of that, and without the cross—if there had been no cross—this world would have been in serious trouble.

One of the things we see when we read Romans 5:12–21 is how devastating Adam's sin was to God's entire creation, as well as to God himself (Genesis 6:5-8). Before Adam's trespass sin and death did not exist in God's perfect world. When Adam sinned, he caused both of those horrors to fall upon the whole creation—sentencing all men to death—and there was nothing anyone could do to prevent that from happening (Hebrews 9:27). Therefore, Adam is the source of death with all its pain, sorrow, and hardships. Christ, on the other hand, is the source of life and justification—with all of its glory, joy, and blessings. Adam's trespass was caused by self-indulgence, and it came with the power to kill and destroy. The free gift of Christ came as the result of one man's self-sacrifice, love, and obedience—It had the power to annul the condemnation that Adam's sin had caused and establish eternal life for all men.

However, there was another problem apart from Adam's trespass that Jesus' cross annulled: the many sins of many men that they had committed themselves—"for all have sinned and fall short of the glory of God" (Romans 3:23). The death sentence that was passed on to all men because of Adam's trespass was immediately taken away without any man having to do anything to make that happen, but the sins a person commits himself, which are forgiven by the same sacrifice that took away Adam's sin, shall only be forgiven by the conditions that God has demanded must be obeyed to receive that forgiveness. Those conditions are belief that Jesus is the Christ, the Son of God (John 8:24), repentance (Luke 13:3, 5), the confession of sin (1 John 1:9) and being baptized by immersion for the forgiveness of sin (Acts 2:38; 8:32–39; 22:16). That is called obeying the gospel (2 Thessalonians 1:6-10).

It is amazing that God would allow one man's sin to condemn the entire creation and sentence all the living to death. It is equally amazing that the grace of God would allow another Man's righteous act of obedience to forgive Adam's trespass and cancel all its consequences—as well as forgiving all other men who had themselves sinned, and especially those who had trespassed in the Old Testament era long before Jesus died on the cross. All forgiveness comes only from the cross of Jesus (John 14:6). Therefore, there is no forgiveness whatsoever without the cross—and the resurrection. Without the cross and the resurrection none of the promises of God could be fulfilled, and all sinners such as David (2 Samuel 12:13) would have perished. David was forgiven of two capital crimes: adultery with his best friend's and general's wife, Bathsheba, and then the murder of her husband to cover his crime. David never offered any sacrifice or sin-offering for his forgiveness, because for David's sin there was no such sacrifice that could be offered; the penalty for his action was death by stoning. But in the mind of God the power of the cross was in effect before he created the world, and it was certainly in effect before Adam or David sinned—but it all depended on Jesus fulfilling his sacrifice on the cross and being raised from the tomb. That is why sinners, such as David, could be forgiven before Jesus actually died on the cross. Peter and Paul both wrote of this truth:

> And if ye call on him as Father, who without respect of persons judgeth according to each man's work, pass the time of your sojourning in fear: knowing that ye were redeemed, not with corruptible things, with silver or gold, from your vain manner of life handed down from your fathers; but with precious blood, as of a lamb without spot, even the blood of Christ: who was foreknown indeed before the foundation of the world, but was manifested at the end of the times for your sake (1 Peter 1:17–20).

Blessed be the God and Father of our Lord Jesus Christ, who hath blessed us with every spiritual blessing in the heavenly places in Christ: even as he chose us in him before the foundation of the world, that we should be holy and without blemish before him in love. (Ephesians 1:3–4)

Unto me, who am less than the least of all saints, was this grace given, to preach unto the Gentiles the unsearchable riches of Christ; and to make all men see what is the dispensation of the mystery which for ages hath been hid in God who created all things; to the intent that now unto the principalities and the powers in the heavenly places might be made known through the church the manifold wisdom of God, according to the eternal purpose which he purposed in Christ Jesus our Lord. (Ephesians 3:8–11)

Paul, a servant of God, and an apostle of Jesus Christ, according to the faith of God's elect, and the knowledge of the truth which is according to godliness, in hope of eternal life, which God, who cannot lie, promised before times eternal. (Titus 1:1–2)

Be not ashamed therefore of the testimony of our Lord, nor of me his prisoner: but suffer hardship with the gospel according to the power of God; who saved us, and called us with a holy calling, not according to our works, but according to his own purpose and grace, which was given us in Christ Jesus before times eternal. (2 Timothy 1:8–9)

The crucifixion took place about 33 A.D., but the power of the cross to restore all things and forgive all sinners was in force before the foundation of the world, even before "times eternal." All the saints in the Old Testament who were forgiven of their sins were forgiven because they tried to live for God by their faith, and by obeying his law. Though their efforts to live for God and atone for their sins required animal sacrifices, their actual forgiveness came only by the way of the cross of Jesus (John 14:6). All of this is why the cross was so critical, so vital, and why, when Jesus was in the garden pleading to his Father for his life and his request was denied, "he said, *Not my will, but thy will be done!*" (Matthew 26:42-44; Mark 14:32-42). All the promises of God: the forgiveness of sin and the restoration of the creation depended on Jesus' cross and resurrection being an accomplished fact.

Jesus came into this world with the express purpose of offering himself as a sacrifice to take away the sins of the world. He came as the Son of God, and the Son of man; he was born of a woman and born under his own law (Galatians 4:4). He was born to a virgin (Isaiah 7:14; Matthew 1:23). He was willing to give up his equality with God to accomplish that. Paul wrote:

> Have this mind in you, which was also in Christ Jesus: who, existing in the form of God, counted not the being on an equality with God a thing to be grasped, but emptied himself, taking the form of a servant, being made in the likeness of men; and being found in fashion as a man, he humbled himself, becoming obedient even unto death, yea, the death of the cross. (Philippians 2:5–8)

Jesus was born to become a man exactly like all other men—with one exception—he was not only the Son of man and the Son of God; he was also Almighty Jehovah God himself (John 1:1–2, 14; Colossians 2:9; Isaiah 9:6; Jeremiah 23:5–6). Hebrews 2:17 says, "Wherefore it behooved him in all things to be made like unto his brethren, that he might become a merciful and faithful high priest in things pertaining to God, to make propitiation for the sins of the people." Jesus was also tempted just like all other men are tempted, but he never sinned. Hebrews 4:15 says, "For we have not a high priest that cannot be touched with the feeling of our infirmities; but one that hath been in all points tempted like as we are, yet without sin."

God does not accept defeat, nor does he tolerate failure, and nothing surprises God. That is the reason why the Almighty does not panic when everything goes wrong and evil things happen. It is ironic, but God knew what Adam and Eve were going to do before he even started his work on the first day of the creation. He knew they would sin against him and that their trespass would condemn his entire world. Therefore, God had a plan to correct all of those problems before they happened. His plan was to abolish the consequence of Adam's trespass, restore the world back to its original beauty and perfection, and offer eternal life to all who had been threatened with death because of Adam's transgression, and *"much more."* Part of the *"much more"* is—the new world of God (God's New Jerusalem, which is the church) would continually and perfectly be protected from sin and all defilement by the blood of Jesus' cross—forever (Matthew 16:18).

God accomplished his plan of salvation in a righteous and holy way by taking the full responsibility for Adam's transgression upon himself, and by paying for it in full by his Son's death on the cross. No sin was overlooked or just forgotten; every sin was punished and paid for by Jesus and his cross. We owed a debt we could not pay; he paid the debt he did not owe. God made that payment himself when he offered up his only begotten Son to be crucified on a cross that took away the sins of the world.

God's plan was to restore the old world which stood condemned by Adam's trespass and make it into a new world. It might have been easier for God to have just annihilated this present evil world and created another one that was perfect—and then keep it that way—instead of trying to repair this world. There are times when buying new is much better than trying to fix something that is worn out or broken. However, God would have considered that a failure, and God does not tolerate failure, nor does he fail. But men do fail, and sometimes even they do not tolerate their own failures. When Thomas Edison was trying to invent the incandescent light bulb, and he had tried one-thousand times to find something that would work for the filament by using different materials—and nothing worked—he was asked: "How does it feel to have a thousand failures?" His response was, "I haven't failed once, I have just found a thousand things that will not work." Vince Lombardy was asked how it felt to lose a ball game. His reply was, "I don't know, I've never lost one, I just ran out of time."

God called his new restored world the kingdom of heaven (Matthew 5:10), the kingdom of God (Mark 1:15), or the church (Matthew 16:18). The writer of the Hebrew letter described the church very clearly when he wrote the following:

> For ye are not come unto a mount that might be touched, and that burned with fire, and unto blackness, and darkness, and tempest, and the sound of a trumpet, and the voice of words; which voice they that heard entreated that no word more should be spoken unto them; for they could not endure that which was enjoined, if even a beast touch the mountain, it shall be stoned; and

so fearful was the appearance, that Moses said, I exceedingly fear and quake: but ye are come unto mount Zion, and unto the city of the living God, the heavenly Jerusalem, and to innumerable hosts of angels, to the general assembly and church of the firstborn who are enrolled in heaven, and to God the Judge of all, and to the spirits of just men made perfect, and to Jesus the mediator of a new covenant, and to the blood of sprinkling that speaketh better than that of Abel. See that ye refuse not him that speaketh. For if they escaped not when they refused him that warned them on earth, much more shall not we escape who turn away from him that warneth from heaven. (Hebrews 12:18–25)

The writer of Hebrews described the church as God views it, and not as men see it. Many men see the church as people and a building, but that is not the church. The church is composed of all the saints who have been called out of the world by the grace of God, and they entered the kingdom of heaven by their faith. The church was also described in John's revelation letter to the Seven Churches of Asia (chapters 21, and 22).

The new heavens and the new earth, or the church, will not allow the devil entrance. It is the perfect place where evil, sin, and death cannot exist. It is where God's children can live with their Father in absolute peace, perfection, and safety—forever. It is the new world wherein dwells righteousness because it shall forever be protected from all defilement by the blood of Jesus' cross. Peter wrote, "But, according to his promise, we look for new heavens and a new earth, wherein dwelleth righteousness" (2 Peter 3:13). That world, the new heavens and the new earth is the eternal dwelling place of the church.

In the beginning when God created the world he gave it to Adam, and Adam became the commander and chief over the entire creation (Genesis 1:27-30): so also has God given his new creation, the kingdom of God, to his saints, his children. Luke wrote, "Yet seek ye his kingdom, and these things shall be added unto you. Fear not, little flock; for it is your Father's good pleasure to give you the kingdom (Luke 12:31-32). It is God's children, Christians, who own the kingdom of God. Have you ever owned a kingdom? Would you like to? Here is a good place to start.

The forgiveness of sin, the resurrection, and the free gift of eternal life is an established fact that is most certain, and it has been assured to all men everywhere by the promise of God, and the Almighty Jehovah God cannot lie. Hebrews 6:13–19 says:

> For when God made promise to Abraham, since he could swear by none greater, he sware by himself saying, Surely blessing I will bless thee, and multiplying I will multiply thee. And thus, having patiently endured, he obtained the promise. For men swear by the greater: and in every dispute of theirs the oath is final for confirmation. Wherein God, being minded to show more abundantly unto the heirs of the promise the immutability of his counsel, interposed with an oath; that by two immutable things, in which it is impossible for God to lie, we may have a strong encouragement, who have fled for refuge to lay hold of the hope set before us: which we have as an anchor of the soul, a hope both sure and stedfast and entering into that which is within the veil.

Therefore, all who believe and obey Jesus and agree to abide in his word (John 8:31–32) and walk in his light (1 John 1:7), shall know the truth and have the promise of the forgiveness of sin and eternal life made sure to them. That is a promise that cannot fail. The two immutable things that establish the promise are: first, the promise itself, and then God's oath that seals the promise. That is the free gift that came by the grace of Jesus (Romans 5:15), and by the abundant mercy and love of the Almighty himself (Romans 5:17).

INTRODUCTION

THE CROSS IS THE most powerful force, and yet it is the most dreaded and feared force that has ever existed. The cross is powerful, beautiful, and wonderful to Christians because it is the result of the love, the mercy, and the grace of God; it is by the way of the cross that men are offered salvation from sin and death and are given eternal life. But the cross is feared and dreaded by the devil and his angels, and by unbelievers, because it is the very force that destroyed their world, and it is the power that shall condemn them to eternal perdition in the day of judgment.

The cross is as powerful as is the creation itself—and it is even more powerful. When the creation was destroyed by the sin of one man, it was the cross of one Man that restored it back to its original perfection and magnificence, just as it was when God created it. That restoration of all things was much more time-consuming, and much more complicated than was the making of the original creation. It took God six days to create the world and there was no opposition. It took God four thousand years to redeem the creation and restore it back into its original perfection and glory after it had been condemned by Adam's sin, and there was great opposition.

The cross is beautiful and powerful to the believer because it saves them from sin, death, and the judgment that is to come, and gives them eternal life. Jesus said, "I am the resurrection, and the life: he that believeth on me, though he die, yet shall he live; and whosoever liveth and believeth on me shall never die. Believest thou this?" (John 11:25–26). That is one of the most beautiful, encouraging, and powerful Scriptures in the Bible. Another is, "For God so loved the world, that he gave his only begotten Son, that whosoever believeth on him should not perish, but have eternal life" (John 3:16).

It was the cross that annulled Adam's sin and abolished its consequence—the consequence being the annihilation of the entire creation and the death of all living creatures. It is the cross that takes away the sting of death, the fear of death, and then offers all men eternal life. It is the cross that makes it bearable for a person to attend the funeral of the one they love the very most, knowing that because of Jesus they shall see that person again, quite alive. What kind of power does it take to overcome death, to annihilate death, or to bring back to life someone who has died? What power could even exist in such a condemned world as the one in which we live that has such power and authority that it could offer the gift of eternal life to all men in a perfect world where death does not exist; where there is no pain, no disease, and nothing can ever go wrong? When a person believes that Jesus is the Christ, the Son of God, and that he died on a cross and was resurrected—and they are baptized and abide in his Word—their sins are forgiven and they are given new a life in a new world, and great things begin to happen (John 8:31–32).

When a person becomes a Christian the first thing that happens is the fear of death and judgment is abolished. It is those two fears that are the most terrifying anxieties a person can experience. All men have some dread of death because they know that someday they must face that king of terrors (Job 18:14), and it is the end of life as they know it in this world. But the fear of losing someone they love dearly, such as their mate or a child, is even more horrifying. It is the cross of Jesus that makes it bearable.

There is the story of an old man who had been happily married for many years; but one day his wife died. He lived next door to a family—one of the family-members was a small lad. One day little Richard saw the old man sitting on his porch, he was broken up, he was crying and trying to endure the pain and agony of losing his wife. The little boy went up to his porch and sat down beside him. Then he climbed up into the old man's lap and just sat there for quite some time. When he returned home his mother asked him, "What were you doing over at David's house for so long?" The lad responded and said, "I just sat on his lap and helped him cry."

Christians should not fear death or the judgment because for them neither one of those horrifying events even exists—because Jesus abolished both of them by his cross and resurrection. Paul wrote, "but hath now been manifested by the appearing of our Saviour Christ Jesus, who abolished death, and brought life and immortality to light through the gospel" (2 Timothy 1:10). Jesus released all Christians from the judgment by taking the sentence of death that they should have experienced upon himself. John wrote:

> For God sent not the Son into the world to judge the world; but that the world should be saved through him. He that believeth on him is not judged: he that believeth not hath been judged already, because he hath not believed on the name of the only begotten Son of God. (John 3:17–18)
>
> Verily, verily, I say unto you, He that heareth my word, and believeth him that sent me, hath eter-

nal life, and cometh not into judgment, but hath passed out of death into life. (John 5:24)

It was by Jesus' death on the cross that God made all Christians just as righteous as He himself is righteous (2 Corinthians 5:21; 1 John 3:7). God also made all Christians just as holy as He is holy (1 Peter 1:16). What more can a Christian ask for? The moment a person is baptized they are relieved from being under law, they are released from the judgment, and they are freed from sin and its curse—which is death—and they immediately enter into perfect eternal life with Jesus, their Lord, their Savior, their Brother (Hebrews 2:11) —and with God, their Father. The cross is the power that made that all possible and delivered us "out of this present evil world" (Galatians 1:3–5) and into the kingdom of God, or into heaven, where we shall be able to meet with all the saints that we have read about in the Bible. We can actually sit down and have all the time in eternity to talk to Enoch, Noah, Abraham, Joseph, Moses, David, the apostles, and even with Jesus himself. We are delivered out of this world and into God's kingdom the very moment we are baptized, not when Jesus comes again the second time to raise the dead and establish the new heavens and the new earth. Paul wrote, "Grace to you and peace from God the Father, and our Lord Jesus Christ, who gave himself for our sins, that he might deliver us out of this present evil world, according to the will of our God and Father: to whom be the glory for ever and ever. Amen" (Galatians 1:3–5).

The cross gives a Christian the power to live without sin— that is, to never have a sin charged against them. John wrote:

> Every one that doeth sin doeth also lawlessness; and sin is lawlessness. And ye know that he was manifested to take away sins; and in him is no sin. Whosoever abideth in him sinneth not: whosoever sinneth hath not seen him, neither knoweth

him. My little children, let no man lead you astray: he that doeth righteousness is righteous, even as he is righteous: he that doeth sin is of the devil; for the devil sinneth from the beginning. To this end was the Son of God manifested, that he might destroy the works of the devil. Whosoever is begotten of God doeth no sin, because his seed abideth in him: and he cannot sin, because he is begotten of God. In this the children of God are manifest, and the children of the devil: whosoever doeth not righteousness is not of God, neither he that loveth not his brother. (1 John 3:4–10)

If any man sees his brother sinning a sin not unto death, he shall ask, and God will give him life for them that sin not unto death. There is a sin unto death: not concerning this do I say that he should make request. All unrighteousness is sin: and there is a sin not unto death. We know that whosoever is begotten of God sinneth not; but he that was begotten of God keepeth himself, and the evil one toucheth him not. We know that we are of God, and the whole world lieth in the evil one. And we know that the Son of God is come, and hath given us an understanding, that we know him that is true, and we are in him that is true, even in his Son Jesus Christ. This is the true God, and eternal life. (1 John 5:16–20)

Both of those Scriptures might be a little difficult to understand, for we know that we do sin no matter how hard we try not to (Romans 3:23; 1 John 1:8–10). However, when we are faithfully living for God, and we are walking in the light (1 John 1:7) and trying our best to not sin—but we sin anyway—the sin we commit is never charged against us. As the Roman letter says, it is not imputed to us (Romans 5:13), for it is immediately nailed to the cross of Jesus and forgiven. Therefore, we are justified, for it is just as if we had never committed the sin in the first place. The implication of the Scriptures that John wrote saying we cannot sin mean we shall never be charged with sin. They also say that the cross makes a Christian perfectly righteous, just as righteous as God himself is righteous. Paul wrote, "Him who knew no sin he made to be sin on our behalf; that we might become the righteousness of God in him" (2 Corinthians 5:21). John wrote, "My little children, let no man lead you astray: he that doeth righteousness is righteous, even as he is righteous" (1 John 3:7). All of that is accomplished by the love of God, by the grace and the mercy of Jesus (Ephesians 2:8–9; Titus 3:4–7), by the power of the Holy Spirit, by the power of the cross, and by our faith.

The cross also makes a Christian just like God. John wrote:

> Behold what manner of love the Father hath bestowed upon us, that we should be called children of God; and such we are. For this cause the world knoweth us not, because it knew him not. Beloved, now are we children of God, and it is not yet made manifest what we shall be. We know that, if he shall be manifested, we shall be like him; for we shall see him even as he is. And every one that hath this hope set on him purifieth himself, even as he is pure. (1 John 3:1–3)

That is the way Adam was when he was originally created in God's image, he was pure and holy because he belonged to God, and he had never sinned. Moses wrote, "And God created man in his own image, in the image of God created he him; male and female created he them" (Genesis 1:27). After a person has sinned, it is the cross of Jesus that recreates them back into that image.

The cross is dreaded and feared by the devil and his evil angels because it is the power that has destroyed them and their world. The cross is also dreaded by unbelievers because it defeats everything they have to hope for, or live for, in the short time they live in this present evil world. No matter how much money a person has, or how many things they possess, or how much they know, or what a troubled-free life they live; —or how high and mighty they are in the social world, the political world, the entertainment world, or the sports world; —it only lasts for the few years they live in this present evil world, and then it's all gone, it's all over forever. Soloman was the richest man who ever lived (Ecclesiastes 2:1-17), and the wisest man who ever lived (1 Kings 3:5-13), and when his years were coming to an end, he said:

> So I hated life, because the work that is wrought under the sun was grievous unto me; for all is vanity and a striving after wind. And I hated all my labor wherein I labored under the sun, seeing that I must leave it unto the man that shall be after me. And who knoweth whether he will be a wise man or a fool? yet will he have rule over all my labor wherein I have labored, and wherein I have showed myself wise under the sun. This also is vanity. (Ecclesiastes 2:17-19).

Paul was a chief leader among his people, the Israelites (Galatians 1:13-14). He was a Hebrew of Hebrews and a Pharisee (Philippians 3:4-7); he had arrived! He gave it all up to become a Christian and an apostle. We can contrast what Soloman said at the end of his life, having lived for the luxuries and pleasures of life; with what Paul said when he knew his end was near, having lived for the Almighty, 2 Timothy 4:6-8:

> For I am already being offered, and the time of my departure is come. I have fought the good fight, I have finished the course, I have kept the faith: henceforth there is laid up for me the crown of righteousness, which the Lord, the righteous judge, shall give to me at that day; and not to me only, but also to all them that have loved his appearing.

> Charge them that are rich in this present world, that they be not highminded, nor have their hope set on the uncertainty of riches, but on God, who giveth us richly all things to enjoy; that they do good, that they be rich in good works, that they be ready to distribute, willing to communicate; laying up in store for themselves a good foundation against the time to come, that they may lay hold on the life which is life indeed. (1 Timothy 6:17-19)

It matters little how great, how rich, or how powerful a person is in this present world, when they die—they lose it all. Death is the great equalizer. When one enters a mortuary and sees two bodies—each one in their own little box—one might be the poorest of the poor, the other the richest of the rich; one might be a beggar, and the other a king; what is the difference in them after death? When they left this world and entered the next, they became quite equal in every respect, the only thing either of them possessed was the little box they were in, and the only difference in them would be: —was one of them a Christian?

There was a very rich man who possessed a mansion with its many antiques and treasures. He had a faithful servant, and over the years he had become quite fond of him. One day the rich man invited his lowly servant into his large house and showed him all of his worldly wealth and treasures. It took some time. The servant said nothing, he just observed. When the tour ended, the rich man said, "Well! what do think about all of this?" All the servant said to his master was, "It must be all of these things that make it so very difficult for you to die." The Christians have no end of life, and no matter how poor they are in this present evil world, the day is soon coming when they shall be the richest of the rich, for they shall own a kingdom, and they shall live in absolute perfection and comfort forever in the house of God, or in his kingdom—a kingdom that they own! When a very poor man dies, he has a great advantage over the richest man who dies; the poor man has absolutely nothing to lose or leave behind. When that transpires the children of God shall own everything God owns, because their Father has given it to them (Luke 12:32; Romans 8:16–17), and the Almighty owns everything. Don't be an unbeliever!

There were two men who had been to a funeral of a very wealthy man. They left the funeral parlor and were standing on a street corner just talking. There was a little boy there playing with his little push-cars—"*zoom, zoom*!" They said one to another, "Man! he was rich, how much was he worth?" "How much did he leave when he died?" They didn't know. The little boy said, "I know how much he left." They said, "ok smart lad, how much?" The little boy looked up at them and he said, "*He left all of it!*" "How much was he worth?" Better, "how much did he have?" All men are worth exactly the same. Jack Benny said, "There are some who are rich, and there are some who have a lot of money." From Adam till the end of time the value of a person cannot be measured by how much he has, who he is, how much he knows; or how high he is in the entertainment world, the sports world, the social world, or the political world. All men are created and given life in the image of God (Genesis 1:26-27), and God is the Father of their spirits (Hebrews 12:9). (That is the part of us that gives us life, John 6:63, and that is the part of us that makes all men of equal value.) We are of such value to God that when we fell away from him because of sin he sent his Son to die on a cross to redeem us and restore us back to life.

It was the cross of Jesus that destroyed all the power the devil held over sin and death. John wrote, "He that doeth sin is of the devil; for the devil sinneth from the beginning. To this end was the Son of God manifested, that he might destroy the works of the devil" (1 John 3:8). When Jesus destroyed the works of the devil with the power of his cross, he took away all the devil's power, and that gave the Christians a great victory with nothing to fear. But the demons, who are Satan's evil angels that fell with him (2 Peter 2:4; Jude 1:6), fear Jesus and his cross above all things, because they have no forgiveness and no redemption (Hebrews 2:16). They knew the exact day that they would be judged, and they greatly feared it. Matthew wrote:

> And when he was come to the other side into the country of the Gadarenes, there met him two possessed with demons, coming forth out of the tombs, exceeding fierce, so that no man could pass by that way. And behold, they cried out, saying, What have we to do with thee, thou Son of God? art thou come hither to torment us before the time? (Matthew 8:28–29)

The reason the demons feared Jesus with such magnum force is because they knew exactly who he was—they knew He was God's holy Son! —They had known Jesus when they had been his holy servants, but that was before they sinned and stood condemned. Luke wrote:

And when the sun was setting, all they that had any sick with divers diseases brought them unto him; and he laid his hands on every one of them, and healed them. And demons also came out from many, crying out, and saying, Thou art the Son of God. And rebuking them, he suffered them not to speak, because they knew that he was the Christ. (Luke 4:40–41)

It is so strange that the rulers of Israel—the Pharisees, the Sadducees, and the doctors of the Law—had no respect for Jesus whatsoever, and they certainly did not fear him. It was their intent to silence him forever by putting him to death. But the demons that had all the power of the devil himself had infinite respect for Jesus, and they feared him with such intense fear that they were terrified by even being in his presence. They certainly did know who He was.

Let us press on and consider what the cross has accomplished. That can be seen in Romans 5:12–21, because it is the cross that annulled Adam's sin (and all sin) and offered eternal life to all men. Romans 5:12–21 is considered one of the more difficult passages of Scripture in the Bible, and that has caused many different "*interpretations.*" But when a person reads it carefully, he can understand what it says without all that difficulty. It says just exactly what it means, it means exactly what it says, and what God wanted people to understand it meant about the consequence of Adam's trespass, and the power of the cross to take it all away. Even Peter had problems understanding the writings of Paul:

And account that the longsuffering of our Lord is salvation; even as our beloved brother Paul also, according to the wisdom given to him, wrote unto you; as also in all his epistles, speaking in them of these things; wherein are some things hard to be understood, which the ignorant and unstedfast wrest, as they do also the other scriptures, unto their own destruction. (2 Peter 3:15–16)

It is encouraging to me to know that an apostle could read the writings of another apostle, like Peter reading Paul's letters, and have as much difficulty understanding them as I have. However, Romans 5:12–21 is not so difficult to understand as it is so very challenging to accept. It is hard to believe that God would proclaim condemnation and death against the whole creation and everyone in it because of the transgression of one man. But that is exactly what Romans 5:12–21 said happened. And yet, that condemnation never fell upon one person, *except Jesus*, because he immediately took it all away with his cross. All of this shall become very clear as we closely examine the contrast between Adam's sin and its consequence—and the free gift of eternal life that came by the way of the cross. Jesus, his cross, and his resurrection have all the power necessary, *and much more*, to completely annihilate Adam's sin and its consequences, and restore all things back to their original perfection and glory.

CHAPTER 1

THE CONTRAST—BETWEEN ADAM'S UNHOLY ACT OF DISOBEDIENCE UNTO DEATH—AND JESUS' RIGHTEOUS ACT OF OBEDIENCE UNTO LIFE (ROMANS 5:15-19)

IT WAS THROUGH ONE man and his trespass against God that sin and death entered the world at a time when love, joy, peace, and fellowship with the Almighty was the established way of life. It was Adam's transgression that changed all of that, threatened to destroy the entire creation, and sentenced all men to death. Had it not been for Jesus and his cross, and his resurrection from the tomb, Adam's sin would have prevailed, and his trespass would have destroyed the whole creation. That would have given Satan exactly what he wanted. However, there was a cross, and there was a resurrection. Therefore, the entire creation has the assured hope of being saved from the consequence of Adam's trespass and restored back to its original beauty and perfection (Romans 8:20–21) —and "much more." By the cross of Jesus all the living who were threatened with death because of Adam's trespass have been given the assured hope of eternal life (1 Corinthians 15:21–22). The crucifixion took place in about the year 33 AD. However, in the mind of God the cross was an established fact before the foundation of the world (1 Peter 1:17–20). Therefore, Adam's trespass was annulled by Jesus and his cross the very moment it was committed.

In Romans 5:12–21, some five times the devastating consequence of Adam's trespass— (A trespass that was caused by his one act of unholy disobedience) —is contrasted against the power of the free gift of God that was established by Jesus and his cross (and His one act of holy and righteous obedience.) What we shall see in that contrast is the deadly capability of Adam's trespass to kill and destroy—weighed against the sanctifying power of the free gift of eternal life that has the power to heal and restore life.

As we travel through Romans 5:12–21, it is necessary to consider three predominant phrases: *the trespass, the free gift, and "much more."* The trespass was Adam's sin. The free gift is the forgiveness of sin and the gift of eternal life (Romans 6:23). The *"much more"* is the free gift that is in every way much more powerful to heal and make alive—than the consequence of Adam's sin was to kill and destroy.

As we view those five contrasts, we shall see that the first part of each verse of Romans 5:15–19 declares the power that Adam's trespass had to condemn, to kill, to destroy, and to sentence all men to death. But the second part of each of those verses avow the counteractive force of the free gift of God—the cross—which has all the power necessary to completely annul the consequence of Adam's trespass and establish a world wherein life and righteousness abide.

The free gift has all of the power of God's grace, and God's grace has no limit (Romans 5:20). That free gift came from the Almighty Jehovah God himself, and it was made possible by the crucifixion and resurrection of his only begotten Son (John 3:16). Therefore, by the contrast we view in Romans 5:12–21, we see the difference between the power of the devil to kill and destroy weighed against the power of God to give life and restore all the things that had been defiled by Adam's transgression. Let us explore that contrast further.

Paul wrote of the first contrast in Romans 5:15, saying, "But not as the trespass, so also is the free gift. For if by the trespass of the one the many died, much more did the grace of God, and the gift by the grace of the one man, Jesus Christ, abound unto the many."

First, the trespass is diametrically opposed to the free gift, for they are exact opposites. All five of the contrasts that we consider shall reflect that assessment. Also, notice how the Scriptures speak exclusively of one man and one trespass—contrasted against one free gift and one act of holy obedience—*and just one.* It was just one man and his one act of unrighteous disobedience that caused the judgment of sin and death to fall upon all men, and it was just one Man and his one act of holy righteous obedience that took it all away and established eternal life.

The one trespass by the one man, Adam, caused the many (meaning all men) (Romans 5:18) to die. When Adam was sentenced to death for his trespass, all men were sentenced to death with him (Romans 5:12; Hebrews 9:27). The very day that all men were sentenced to death was the day Adam sinned.

Adam's transgression was caused by the evil influence of Satan. It had the power to kill and destroy. The free gift came by the abundant grace and mercy of God; it has the power to take away Adam's sin and offer eternal life to all men who had been threatened with death because of Adam's trespass. The free gift also has the power and the authority to forgive all men of their own sins: (the sins they themselves had committed, and still do commit). It took the cross, the death of God's only begotten Son to make that free gift possible.

This alone shows the value and the power of the free gift. The free gift is free because there is no price on earth that can purchase it, not with silver or gold (1 Peter 1:17–20). It is a *free* gift, not just a gift, because the one who receives it cannot compensate the giver in any way. Some gifts are given because the one who gives them expects a favor in return. Not so with our heavenly Father. Even for the Almighty there was no other way to take away the sins of the world and offer salvation to all men but by the way of the cross, which is the very way God accomplished it.

Our loving God put all of that together and made it happen. John wrote, "For God so loved the world, that he gave his only begotten Son, that whosoever believeth on him should not perish, but have eternal life" (John 3:16). Paul wrote about how it was the grace and mercy of God that made the forgiveness of sin and the free gift of eternal life possible. God's Grace is the Almighty's power to give us many wonderful and beautiful blessings that we do not deserve, such as the forgiveness of sin and eternal life. God's Mercy is his power that grants reprieve from the punishment we do deserve, such as eternal death. Justice is receiving exactly what we do deserve. It was the free gift that came as a result of the crucifixion and resurrection of Jesus that made grace and mercy possible—it is the law that established justice. The free gift is eternal life (Romans 6:23). Paul wrote of the power of the cross, and of the power of the free gift of God's grace and mercy, when he said:

> And you did he make alive, when ye were dead through your trespasses and sins, wherein ye once walked according to the course of this world, according to the prince of the powers of

the air, of the spirit that now worketh in the sons of disobedience; among whom we also all once lived in the lust of our flesh, doing the desires of the flesh and of the mind, and were by nature children of wrath, even as the rest:—but God, being rich in mercy, for his great love wherewith he loved us, even when we were dead through our trespasses, made us alive together with Christ (by grace have ye been saved), and raised us up with him, and made us to sit with him in the heavenly places, in Christ Jesus: that in the ages to come he might show the exceeding riches of his grace in kindness toward us in Christ Jesus: for by grace have ye been saved through faith; and that not of yourselves, it is the gift of God; not of works, that no man should glory. (Ephesians 2:1–9)

For we also once were foolish, disobedient, deceived, serving divers lusts and pleasures, living in malice and envy, hateful, hating one another. But when the kindness of God our Saviour, and his love toward man, appeared, not by works done in righteousness, which we did ourselves, but according to his mercy he saved us, through the washing of regeneration and renewing of the Holy Spirit, which he poured out upon us richly, through Jesus Christ our Saviour; that, being justified by his grace, we might be made heirs according to the hope of eternal life. (Titus 3:3–7)

For while we were yet weak, in due season Christ died for the ungodly. For scarcely for a righteous man will one die: for peradventure for the good man some one would even dare to die. But God commendeth his own love toward us, in that, while we were yet sinners, Christ died for us. Much more then, being now justified by his blood, shall we be saved from the wrath of God through him. For if, while we were enemies, we were reconciled to God through the death of his Son, much more, being reconciled, shall we be saved by his life; and not only so, but we also rejoice in God through our Lord Jesus Christ, through whom we have now received the reconciliation. (Romans 5:6–11)

The next contrast is in Romans 5:16, where it is written, "And not as through one that sinned, so is the gift: for the judgment came of one unto condemnation, but the free gift came of many trespasses unto justification." First, Adam was a sinner, and the trespass he committed by eating the fruit of the forbidden tree was what made him a sinner. It was Adam's transgression that caused the judgment of condemnation to fall upon him, and upon all men. The free gift that Jesus offers to all men allowing them to escape the condemnation of Adam's trespass came by the grace of one Man and his one act of holy righteous obedience, *and he was no sinner*—Jesus was perfect and holy in all of his ways (Hebrews 7:26-27). He is our Savior and our High Priest, and he had no sin (Hebrews 4:15). The Hebrew letter says:

For such a high priest became us, holy, guileless, undefiled, separated from sinners, and made higher than the heavens; who needeth not daily, like those high priests, to offer up sacrifices, first for his own sins, and then for the sins of the people: for this he did once for all, when he offered up himself. For the law appointeth men high priests, having infirmity; but the word of the oath, which was after the law, appointeth a Son, perfected for evermore. (Hebrews 7:26–28)

There is a great contrast between Adam and Christ—and between Adam's sin (and its consequences unto death) —and the free gift of eternal life that Jesus offers to all men (with its infinite benefits and blessings). Adam was one man who committed one trespass, and that one trespass condemned the whole creation and everyone in it. Jesus' one act of righteous obedience annulled Adam's sin and its consequences, and with that one sacrifice Jesus paid in full for all the damage Adam's sin had caused. That payment, or ransom, was paid in full by the blood of the cross. But there were other sins that had been committed by many other men, and when Jesus annulled the consequence of Adam's trespass, he also canceled the punishment that was due to fall upon all men for their own sins, and he offered forgiveness to all who had themselves sinned against God. When Adam sinned, the whole world stood condemned by his one trespass. When Jesus died on the cross, he sanctified the whole creation and took away Adam's sin—and its consequences—and by his death and resurrection he took away all the sins of the world (John 1:29). Then he offered eternal life to all who would accept his promise by believing that he is the Christ, the Son of God. That is the contrast.

The third contrast is found in Romans 5:17, where it is written, "For if, by the trespass of the one, death reigned through the one; much more shall they that receive the abundance of grace and of the gift of righteousness reign in life through the one, even Jesus Christ." It is terrifying, it is horrifying, and it is unimaginable to even try to begin to understand the devastating power of sin. The most powerful force in the universe is the power of the Almighty who spoke the creation into its existence. The second most powerful force is the power of Satan to do everything possible to destroy the works of God. The power of Satan is sin. Sin, death, and temptation are the only powers Satan has, but even so those evil forces are sufficient for him to accomplish his purpose, unless he is resisted (James 4:7–10). It is sin that gives death its terrifying strength, and without sin death has no sting, and death has no force. Paul wrote:

> But when this corruptible shall have put on incorruption, and this mortal shall have put on immortality, then shall come to pass the saying that is written, Death is swallowed up in victory. O death, where is thy victory? O death, where is thy sting? The sting of death is sin; and the power of sin is the law: but thanks be to God, who giveth us the victory through our Lord Jesus Christ. (1 Corinthians 15:54–57)

To understand how powerful sin is, all we must do is view the consequence of the one sin that Adam committed, and his one sin was eating the fruit of the forbidden tree. That was the moment when sin and death entered the world and passed on to all men, and that was the moment when the reign of death began. It is amazing that one man's sin could sentence all men to death and cause a reign of death to fall upon the entire world; it is even more astonishing that death could be turned into a victory; but that is exactly what happened when Jesus died on the cross and was resurrected to new life on the third day after his crucifixion. The victory is this: The very force that Satan intended to use to destroy all the living—death—was turned into the greatest of all victories by being the very means by which God would deliver his children out of this present evil world (Galatians 1:3–4), and bestow upon them the free gift of eternal life in another world. The only escape we have from this present evil world so we can enter the next world is by death. That is, our spirits leaving our bodies, so in our spirits we can return to God to live with him in the new heavens and the new earth—forever. That new heaven and new earth is the new spiritual world that God has created for us. In that world we shall have a new spiritual body which shall live quite well and comfortable in a spiritual world (1 Corinthians 15:42-44). A flesh and blood body cannot enter that world (1 Corinthians 15:50). That blessing was established for all men by Christ annulling Adam's sin, and the death he caused by his disobedience, and turn it into a victory by his resurrection. What strange, ironic, and powerful ways God has to defeat the devil, and to humiliate him by using his own power and his own ways to destroy him.

Before Adam sinned the whole world was at peace, and there was no need for any kind of a victory—for there were no evil forces to conquer. All men, and even the animals were at peace with each other, and the whole world was at peace with the Almighty (Genesis 1:31). But about 1,656 years after God created the world men's trespasses became so great that God could no longer tolerate the way they lived (Genesis 6:5–7), and so he destroyed the entire world with a flood. It was after the flood that the relationship of peace between men and animals ended. Moses wrote:

> And the fear of you and the dread of you shall be upon every beast of the earth, and upon every bird of the heavens; With all wherewith the ground teemeth, and all the fishes of the sea, into your hand are they delivered. Every moving thing that liveth shall be food for you; As the green herb have I given you all. (Genesis 9:2–3)

It was Adam's sin that caused enmity between men and God, between men themselves, between nations, and even between men and animals. That was the moment when all living creatures

47

were no longer vegetarians. Men started using animals for food and animals started eating each other. It was Adam's reign of death that was the cause of all of that and threatened the entire world with the extinction of all living creatures. That included the animal world, despite animals having no sin. It is appalling to see how animals struggle and die because of one man's sin. Whales and dolphins are air breathing animals, and they are among the most intelligent creatures to which God has given life. There are occasions when their life is coming to an end and they know they are going to die, they will swim rapidly toward land and beach themselves so they will not die by drowning, because for them to die by drowning is terrifying and painful. Animals will struggle to live just as humans do, because they want to live as intensely as we want to live.

There was an occasion in southern Mexico near Zihuantanejo where a whale had become entangled in fish nets. She was a young whale, and she was struggling for her life. She was going to drown if something wasn't done. There was a small boat of fishermen that immediately went to her aid. It took some time, but they cut the animal free from the net, and from her agony. For over two hours that animal swam around their little boat and was diving and waving her tail in thanksgiving to the men who had saved her life. Even animals are grateful for the aid they receive, even though sometimes they might not express it. God is great!

It is necessary to consider the reign of death. It ruled over the world from the time Adam sinned until the time of Moses (Romans 5:14). What was it? What could be done to take away the reign of death? Why did the reign of death end with the coming of Moses? The reign of death was the condemning force that Adam caused by his trespass, and it ruled over all the living sentencing them to death (Hebrews 9:27). When men and little babies experience physical death, they do not die because they have sinned, they die because Adam sinned.

Adam's transgression also introduced the knowledge of good and evil into the world. Before Adam and Eve ate the fruit of the forbidden tree they were as innocent as little children— because they were little children. When they lived in their garden they were both naked, and they were not ashamed. Evidently there must have been a reason they should have been ashamed, but they did not know it until immediately after they ate the fruit of the Tree of Knowledge, and then they were ashamed. The knowledge of good and evil immediately entered the minds of Adam and Eve the very moment they sinned. That knowledge also passed on to all men, and that is a fact expressed in other literature. It is in our Declaration of Independence. Thomas Jefferson wrote, "We hold these truths to be self-evident, that all men are created equal, that they are endowed by their Creator with certain unalienable Rights, that among these are Life, Liberty and the pursuit of Happiness." To be *"self-evident"* means they were not learned, they were inherent in a person from the time they were born. The fact that all tribes and clans, no matter how primitive they are, wear loin cloths to cover their nakedness proves they instinctively know that such is necessary, because God revealed it to them.

It was by the coming of the knowledge of good and evil that men were forced to live by their conscience. When they knew what was right and did not do it, or when they knew what was wrong and they did it anyway, they sinned (James 4:17). During the time there was no law, and before the knowledge of good and evil came into the minds of all men, sin was not possible. Adam sinned by breaking the one law God gave him, but if there had there been no law, there would have been no sin.

Adam's transgression caused the knowledge of good and evil to pass on to all men just as sin and death passed on to all men. As a result, after Adam sinned, all men knew instinctively that some things were right and other things were wrong. To illustrate that we can look at the life of a young man who did not live under law but still maintained very high moral standards. His name was Joseph. Joseph was the eleventh son of Jacob, or Israel. Joseph maintained such high standards of honesty and morality that God blessed him greatly, his father loved him dearly, but his brothers hated him profoundly. They despised him so intensely that they were going to kill him, but instead they had an opportunity to sell him to some Ishmaelites for twenty pieces of silver (Genesis 37:15–35). Jesus was sold for thirty pieces of silver (Matthew 26:14-16).

The Ishmaelites took Joseph to Egypt and sold him to Potiphar, who was a high-ranking officer in Pharaoh's service. He was the captain of the guard (Genesis 37:36). Joseph performed so well as Potiphar's servant that Potiphar made him lord over his entire house, and that all transpired because it was God who was blessing Joseph (Genesis 39:1–6). However, Potiphar was away from home much of the time, and Potiphar's wife had sexual desires that were not being fulfilled, so she looked to Joseph to fulfill them (Genesis 39:7-8). Joseph, being of high moral quality and knowing that adultery was wrong, refused to cooperate. Joseph's response to such offers by such an attractive woman—especially during the time Joseph lived—was quite unusual (Genesis, chapter 38). Potiphar's wife tried to seduce Joseph day by day, and Joseph's final response was:

> Behold, my master knoweth not what is with me in the house, and he hath put all that he hath into my hand: he is not greater in this house than I; neither hath he kept back anything from me but thee, because thou art his wife: how then can I do this great wickedness, and sin against God? And it came to pass, as she spake to Joseph day by day, that he hearkened not unto her, to lie by her, or to be with her. (Genesis 39:8–10)

There was no law against adultery during the time Joseph lived because there was no law, but adultery was still an evil trespass against the Almighty, and it was sin. Joseph knew adultery was wrong, and he knew it instinctively by the knowledge of good and evil that he had dwelling within him, and he conducted himself accordingly. As a result of his high moral standards and his love for the Almighty, Joseph became the ruler of all Egypt (Genesis 41:37-44).

It is necessary to consider the consequences of the reign of death. Death ruled over all the living from the time of Adam to the time of Moses (Romans 5:14), and during that period of time there was no law, and when there was no law sin was not imputed against the one who had sinned. Paul wrote, "for until the law sin was in the world; but sin is not imputed when there is no law" (Romans 5:13). Nevertheless, there was a way that the men who sinned during that period of time were still held accountable for their trespasses—it was by the law of their conscience. Paul wrote:

> For when Gentiles that have not the law do by nature the things of the law, these, not having the law, are the law unto themselves; in that they show the work of the law written in their hearts, their conscience bearing witness therewith, and their thoughts one with another accusing or else excusing them in the day when God shall judge the secrets of men, according to my gospel, by Jesus Christ. (Romans 2:12–16)

It was by instinctively comprehending the law of the knowledge of good and evil that held men accountable for their trespasses. When there was no written or established law, a person was judged by how carefully they tried to do what they knew what was right and avoid doing what was wrong—all according to their knowledge of good and evil, as their conscience guided them. That is the way Joseph lived, and therefore Joseph lived without sin. Joseph was sinless, just as was Enoch, the seventh son from Adam was sinless—he walked with God (Genesis 5:21-24). It was not that they never committed sin (and maybe they hadn't)—it was because of their lifestyle in trying to obey God in all ways and not sin that is the reason sin was never imputed to them. So also it is with us to this very day.

Death reigned for about 2,575 years, which was about the period of time between Adam and Moses. But death only reigned until Moses received the Law of God on Mount Sinai, and that ended the reign of death. That is the time the reign of grace began. That is what the last two verses of Romans chapter 5 say. Paul wrote, "And the law came in besides, that the trespass might abound; but where sin abounded, grace did abound more exceedingly: that, as sin reigned in death, even so might grace reign through righteousness unto eternal life through Jesus Christ our Lord" (Romans 5:20-21). When the Law was given it exposed sin for how evil it truly was. The Law also declared very clearly what was right, what was wrong, the penalty for disobedience, and how God wanted men to live.

With the giving of the Law men received a way by which they could live well pleasing to the Almighty, and the Law directed them in that way of life. When men lived under the Law of Moses, they knew most certainly what was right, what was wrong, and what to do when sin occurred. When men lived under the Law, and they kept the Law, they did not sin, and when they did not sin, they lived. In fact—they were rewarded with the gift of life (Leviticus 18:4–5; Ezekiel 20:11; Romans 10:5). When men broke the Law they sinned, but by the grace of God there were sacrifices they could offer to have their sin forgiven and be restored back into life and fellowship with God. It was by the grace of God that the Law directed men in how the Almighty wanted them to live, and to provide for the forgiveness of sin when the Law was broken. By the grace of God when a man sinned and faced death, an animal could die in his place so the man could live—that allowed the sinner to see how serious his sin was; they must watch the animal die, or kill the animal themselves for what they had done. What a wonderful blessing it is to know that when a person sins, he has a way to be forgiven of his trespass, and a way to be exonerated and restored back to life, and back into fellowship with the Father. It is a blessing to know that when sin abounds, and it seems there is just no way out of it, grace abounds even more exceedingly, and it allows a person to be delivered from the consequences of sin, which is death. The sacrifice that accomplished all of that for the Christians was the blood of the cross of our Savior, Jesus.

It was Christ and his cross that abolished the reign of death and destroyed that king of terrors forever (Job 18:14). Jesus ended the reign of death by facing that terror himself when he died on the cross, but when he was raised from the dead on the third day, he created the reign of life. Jesus said:

> I am the resurrection, and the life: he that believeth on me, though he die, yet shall he live; and whosoever liveth and believeth on me shall never die. Believest thou this? (John 11:25–26)

> For God so loved the world, that he gave his only begotten Son, that whosoever believeth on him should not perish, but have eternal life. For God sent not the Son into the world to judge the world; but that the world should be saved through him. He that believeth on him is not judged: he that believeth not hath been judged already, because he hath not believed on the name of the only begotten Son of God. (John 3:16–18)

Verily, verily, I say unto you, He that heareth my word, and believeth him that sent me, hath eternal life, and cometh not into judgment, but hath passed out of death into life. Verily, verily, I say unto you, The hour cometh, and now is, when the dead shall hear the voice of the Son of God; and they that hear shall live. For as the Father hath life in himself, even so gave he to the Son also to have life in himself: and he gave him authority to execute judgment, because he is a son of man. Marvel not at this: for the hour cometh, in which all that are in the tombs shall hear his voice, and shall come forth; they that have done good, unto the resurrection of life; and they that have done evil, unto the resurrection of judgment. (John 5:24–29)

For I am come down from heaven, not to do mine own will, but the will of him that sent me. And this is the will of him that sent me, that of all that which he hath given me I should lose nothing, but should raise it up at the last day. For this is the will of my Father, that every one that beholdeth the Son, and believeth on him, should have eternal life; and I will raise him up at the last day. The Jews therefore murmured concerning him, because he said, I am the bread which came down out of heaven. And they said, Is not this Jesus, the son of Joseph, whose father and mother we know? how doth he now say, I am come down out of heaven? Jesus answered and said unto them, Murmur not among yourselves. No man can come to me, except the Father that sent me draw him: and I will raise him up in the last day. It is written in the prophets, And they shall all be taught of God. Every one that hath heard from the Father, and hath learned, cometh unto me. Not that any man hath seen the Father, save he that is from God, he hath seen the Father. Verily, verily, I say unto you, He that believeth hath eternal life. I am the bread of life. Your fathers ate the manna in the wilderness, and they died. This is the bread which cometh down out of heaven, that a man may eat thereof, and not die. I am the living bread which came down out of heaven: if any man eat of this bread, he shall live for ever: yea and the bread which I will give is my flesh, for the life of the world. The Jews therefore strove one with another, saying, How can this man give us his flesh to eat? Jesus therefore said unto them, Verily, verily, I say unto you, Except ye eat the flesh of the Son of man and drink his blood, ye have not life in yourselves. He that eateth my flesh and drinketh my blood hath eternal life: and I will raise him up at the last day. For my flesh is meat indeed, and my blood is drink indeed. He that eateth my flesh and drinketh my blood abideth in me, and I in him. As the living Father sent me, and I live because of the Father; so he that eateth me, he also shall live because of me. This is the bread which came down out of heaven: not as the fathers ate, and died; he that eateth this bread shall live for ever. (John 6:38–58)

The choice is ours. We have the right to choose between the reign of death and the reign of life—if we chose the reign of death, it is because we love this present evil world more than we love the kingdom of God; or because we just do not believe the teachings of Christ are all that important. Perhaps we just do not believe that death holds any power over one after he dies. (But it does!) That is the position of an unbeliever. There is another choice we can make. We also have the right to believe God and enter his kingdom by faith and obedience, and with that choice we will leave the reign of death and enter the reign of life, ultimately living forever.

The next contrast we shall view is in Romans 5:18. "So then as through one trespass the judgment came unto all men to condemnation; even so through one act of righteousness the free gift came unto all men to justification of life." It was one trespass that was committed by one man that caused the condemnation of death to fall upon all men. When Adam sinned and stood condemned for his trespass, the entire creation and all men were condemned with him, and there was nothing that any man could do to prevent that from happening. But there was another Man— and just one Man—who could prevent that from happening. That Man who is called the Christ is much greater than Adam, for he is no sinner—he is righteous. It was that one Man's act of righteousness that annulled Adam's act of unrighteousness and declared justification to life for all men. That Man, whose righteous act of obedience saved all men from sin and death, and gave them life, is called Jesus. It was his act of righteous obedience by going to the cross to suffer death by crucifixion that paid in full for Adam's trespass and took away all the sins of the world, and that included Adam's sin (John 1:29).

Jesus' one act of righteousness nullified Adam's sin unconditionally. Just as Adam's sin condemned all men and made all men sinners unconditionally, so also the cross of Jesus unconditionally and immediately took away Adam's sin and brought justification of life to all men. What a difference the cross makes! However, and this is very important: the sins that men commit themselves are also forgiven by Jesus' act of righteousness, but that forgiveness is not unconditional—it is most certainly conditional. For men to receive forgiveness for their own sins (the sins that they themselves have committed) they must repent (Luke 13:3), believe in Jesus (John 8:24), abide in his Word (John 8:31–32), and be baptized (Mark 16:15-16; Acts 2:37-38; Acts 22:16).

The next contrast is found in Romans 5:19. "For as through the one man's disobedience the many were made sinners, even so through the obedience of the one shall the many be made righteous." Adam disobeyed his Father when he ignored his command to not eat of the fruit of the forbidden tree, and he ate of it anyway, and he sinned. That was Adam's one act of disobedience that made him a sinner, and it also made all men sinners. There was nothing that any man could do to prevent being made a sinner by Adam's disobedience. On the other hand, it was the obedience of another Man who is called Jesus that made all men righteous. Just as Adam's disobedience made all men sinners—without anything that any man could do to prevent that from happening—so also the obedience of the one Man, Jesus, made all men righteous, and there was nothing any man must do to receive that free gift. That means that no one, and certainly not babies, must be baptized to be forgiven of Adam's sin. All of that transpired with no lapse of time between the two events. The very moment that all men were made sinners by Adam's disobedience they were instantly made righteous by Jesus' one act of obedience. That transpired because the cross was an established fact before the foundation of the world (1 Peter 1:18-29). So, if that is the way it happened, why did it need to be recorded in the Bible? It was recorded so all men could see how sin originated, how evil, deadly, and serious sin is, the evil consequences of sin, and the appalling price that was required to pay for all the damage and devastation sin had caused. Adam's sin made all men sinners, destroyed the creation, and sentenced all men to death (Romans 8:18-23). Jesus righteous act of obedience—the cross—was the price he and his Father paid to restore the creation back to its original glory and perfection, and restore life to all men.

It is not easy to understand the difference between the consequence of Adam's sin (why all men were sentenced to death because one man sinned)—and the consequence of the sins that other men commit when it seems some of those sins are much more serious than Adam's sin—eating a piece of fruit from a forbidden tree. The difference is: —when Adam sinned, sin and death did not exist, and so Adam was the first man to trespass against the law of God, and sin. Adam was the source of sin and death with all the pain, the agony, the sorrow, and the horror that is associated with it. Therefore, his sin had extremely serious consequences because he was the cause of sin and death. The wages of sin is death, but for Adam's trespass that wage was not disbursed to Adam alone—when Adam sinned he condemned himself, his entire human family, and everything he possessed, and God had given him the entire creation. Therefore, Adam's transgression condemned the whole world and everyone in it. Why God did it that way only he knows, but Adam and the world in which he lived were just one united entity, and when any part of it became contaminated, it all stood condemned.

The penalty for Adam's sin, and the punishment that was decreed against all men for the sins they themselves have committed was the same: death! "The wages of sin is death" (Romans 6:23). It is not easy to understand why Adam's sin condemned everything God had created, but the many sins that many men had committed condemned only the person who had sinned. Ezekiel wrote:

> The soul that sinneth, it shall die: the son shall
> not bear the iniquity of the father, neither shall
> the father bear the iniquity of the son; the righ-
> teousness of the righteous shall be upon him, and

the wickedness of the wicked shall be upon him. (Ezekiel 18:20)

In Adam's case that was not so, because Adam was the first sinner, and he brought sin and death into a world where neither of those terrible things existed.

Another reason Adam's disobedience was recorded in the Bible, even though it was annulled and nailed to the cross the very moment it was committed, is because Adam's sin had serious consequences that still remain in this world today. The leftover consequences of Adam's trespass, such as diseases, physical death, and the horrible way that the world we all live in continually suffers from famines, pestilence, wars, earthquakes, plagues, terrifying storms—and other such things—did not exist until Adam sinned. All of those disasters were caused by that one man's sin (Genesis 3:17–19). We could never know why people must die, and why the world is in such a terrible mess, unless we were informed that it was Adam's sin that caused it all. Since Adam's sin had almost destroyed the creation, the sins that many men had committed had nothing left to destroy, except the soul of the person who committed the sin.

CHAPTER 2

THE ORIGIN OF SIN AND DEATH—THE EVIL FORCES THAT CONDEMNED GOD'S PERFECT WORLD (Romans 5:12–14)

IT WAS THROUGH ONE man, Adam, that sin came into God's perfect world, and with sin came the devastating force of death. "The wages of sin is death" (Romans 6:23). Before Adam sinned, neither of those terrifying threats even existed. Paul wrote:

> Therefore, as through one man sin entered into the world, and death through sin; and so death passed unto all men, for that all sinned: —for until the law sin was in the world; but sin is not imputed when there is no law. Nevertheless death reigned from Adam until Moses, even over them that had not sinned after the likeness of Adam's transgression, who is a figure of him that was to come. (Romans 5:12–14)

Sin is rebellion against God—sin is breaking the law of God, and it is also breaking God's heart in the process (Genesis 6:5–6). Sin is lawlessness. John wrote, "Every one that doeth sin doeth also lawlessness; and sin is lawlessness" (1 John 3:4). Death is a separation (James 2:26); physical death is the separation of the spirit and the soul from the body, spiritual death is the separation of the spirit and the soul from God. James wrote, "For as the body apart from the spirit is dead, even so faith apart from works is dead" (James 2:26). David wrote in the book of Psalms:

> A perverse heart shall depart from me: I will know no evil thing. Whoso privily slandereth his neighbor, him will I destroy: Him that hath a high look and a proud heart will I not suffer. Mine eyes shall be upon the faithful of the land, that they may dwell with me: He that walketh in a perfect way, he shall minister unto me. He that worketh deceit shall not dwell within my house: He that speaketh falsehood shall not be established before mine eyes. Morning by morning will I destroy all the wicked of the land; to cut off all the workers of iniquity from the city of Jehovah. (Psalms 101:4–8)

Death is the punishment that God decreed against sin. Paul wrote, "For the wages of sin is death; but the free gift of God is eternal life in Christ Jesus our Lord" (Romans 6:23). What a tremendous and powerful force sin and death are; they have the power to destroy the entire creation and sentence every living creature to death—And what a powerful counterforce it would take to abolish such a thing as death—but that is exactly what Jesus did with his cross and his resurrection. Paul wrote:

Be not ashamed therefore of the testimony of our Lord, nor of me his prisoner: but suffer hardship with the gospel according to the power of God; who saved us, and called us with a holy calling, not according to our works, but according to his own purpose and grace, which was given us in Christ Jesus before times eternal, but hath now been manifested by the appearing of our Saviour Christ Jesus, who abolished death, and brought life and immortality to light through the gospel. (2 Timothy 1:8–10)

It took six days for God establish his creation and he was well pleased with what he had accomplished; it was beautiful and prefect. Moses wrote in Genesis, "And God saw everything that he had made, and, behold, it was very good. And there was evening and there was morning, the sixth day" (Genesis 1:31). When we view the six days of the creation, and the seventh day on which God rested, we can see the world that God had in his mind from the very beginning (Revelation 4:11), and the world he gave to his son, Adam. We can also see why God loved his new world so very much. Everything God created was perfectly thought out, masterfully made, beautiful, and a testament to the Almighty's engineering skills and workmanship. God is perfect, and he would not tolerate imperfection in anything he made.

It was on the sixth day God created the animals and man, Adam. Adam was given only one law to obey; it was very clear, and very plain:

And Jehovah God took the man, and put him into the garden of Eden to dress it and to keep it. And Jehovah God commanded the man, saying, Of every tree of the garden thou mayest freely eat: but of the tree of the knowledge of good and evil, thou

shalt not eat of it: for in the day that thou eatest
thereof thou shalt surely die. (Genesis 2:15–17)

Adam deliberately violated the only commandment God had
given him, and he sinned. His trespass immediately brought sin
into the world, and with his disobedience came death. Probably
Adam and Eve did not know what death was since nothing had
ever died, but they must have understood it was a horrible experience for anything to have to die. Adam and Eve found out what
death was when they ate the fruit of the forbidden tree and their
eyes were opened, revealing to them they were naked—and God
had to kill an animal and take its skin to cover their nakedness.
Moses wrote, "And Jehovah God made for Adam and for his wife
coats of skins, and clothed them" (Genesis 3:21).

Adam ate the fruit of the forbidden tree, and the very day
he ate of it he died spiritually, for he hid himself from the presence of God (Genesis 3:8), and he was separated from his Father
when he was driven from the garden, and all because of his sin.
Moses wrote:

> And Jehovah God said, Behold, the man is become
> as one of us, to know good and evil; and now, lest
> he put forth his hand, and take also of the tree of
> life, and eat, and live for ever—therefore Jehovah
> God sent him forth from the garden of Eden, to
> till the ground from whence he was taken. So he
> drove out the man; and he placed at the east of
> the garden of Eden the Cherubim, and the flame
> of a sword which turned every way, to keep the
> way of the tree of life. (Genesis 3:22–24)

Adam suffered the death sentence of both physical death and
spiritual death the very day he sinned. It was on that day his
body began to age, to deteriorate, and he started to die a physical

death, and 930 years later that his body died (Genesis 5:5). But Adam did not just die alone—he condemned the entire creation to death by his rebellious action, and that included the entire human family. It was Jesus' cross and resurrection that fully rectified that problem, restored the creation back to God, reinstated life to all those who had been sentenced to death by Adam's sin, and that all transpired the very moment Adam sinned. That is the power of the cross.

When God saw what Adam and Eve had done, and that they had hidden themselves from his presence because they were naked, he asked them if they had eaten of the tree. They did not deny the crime they had committed, but they did pass the blame for their disobedience on to another. Adam blamed the woman God had given him. Eve blamed the serpent for tempting her and deceiving her. The serpent did not have a leg to stand on, for he could do nothing but plead guilty. Moses wrote:

> And Jehovah God called unto the man, and said unto him, Where art thou? And he said, I heard thy voice in the garden, and I was afraid, because I was naked; and I hid myself. And he said, Who told thee that thou wast naked? Hast thou eaten of the tree, whereof I commanded thee that thou shouldest not eat? And the man said, The woman whom thou gavest to be with me, she gave me of the tree, and I did eat. And Jehovah God said unto the woman, What is this thou hast done? And the woman said, The serpent beguiled me, and I did eat. And Jehovah God said unto the serpent, Because thou hast done this, cursed art thou above all cattle, and above every beast of the field; upon thy belly shalt thou go, and dust shalt thou eat all the days of thy life: and I will put enmity between thee and the woman, and between thy seed

and her seed: he shall bruise thy head, and thou shalt bruise his heel. Unto the woman he said, I will greatly multiply thy pain and thy conception; in pain thou shalt bring forth children; and thy desire shall be to thy husband, and he shall rule over thee. And unto Adam he said, Because thou hast hearkened unto the voice of thy wife, and hast eaten of the tree, of which I commanded thee, saying, Thou shalt not eat of it: cursed is the ground for thy sake; in toil shalt thou eat of it all the days of thy life; thorns also and thistles shall it bring forth to thee; and thou shalt eat the herb of the field; in the sweat of thy face shalt thou eat bread, till thou return unto the ground; for out of it wast thou taken: for dust thou art, and unto dust shalt thou return. (Genesis 3:9–19)

God condemned the serpent for his evil deed, but it was not just the serpent that suffered that curse; the serpent was just a tool the devil used. He was most likely a beautiful creature until after he suffered his curse. That is when he lost his limbs and was forced to crawl on the ground like present-day snakes move about. It was Satan himself that suffered that curse, and before that time Satan was a free being and serving God faithfully. Satan was created to be a cherub, and the cherubim were the highest and most glorious servants that God had. It was the cherubim (more than one) that God stationed at the entrance to the Garden of Eden to protect it from intruders (Genesis 3:24), and to protect the way of the tree of life. That included forbidding Satan—a cherub himself—from entering the garden.

So, who was Satan, or the devil? There is very little written about Satan and his origin, but there is one passage of scripture in the book of Ezekiel that helps us understand a little more about who he was and where he came from. In his letter, Ezekiel pronounced a lamentation over the king of Tyre. However, his lamentation did not relate to that king at all, but it did relate perfectly to Satan. That lamentation is found in Ezekiel 28:11–19, and those verses of Scripture vividly describe who Satan was and where he came from:

> Moreover the word of Jehovah came unto me, saying, Son of man, take up a lamentation over the king of Tyre, and say unto him, Thus saith the Lord Jehovah: Thou sealest up the sum, full of wisdom, and perfect in beauty. Thou wast in Eden, the garden of God; every precious stone was thy covering, the sardius, the topaz, and the diamond, the beryl, the onyx, and the jasper, the sapphire, the emerald, and the carbuncle, and gold: the workmanship of thy tabrets and of thy pipes was in thee; in the day that thou wast created they were prepared. Thou wast the anointed cherub that covereth: and I set thee, so that thou wast upon the holy mountain of God; thou hast walked up and down in the midst of the stones of fire. Thou wast perfect in thy ways from the day that thou wast created, till unrighteousness was found in thee. By the abundance of thy traffic they filled the midst of thee with violence, and thou hast sinned: therefore have I cast thee as profane out of the mountain of God; and I have destroyed thee, O covering cherub, from the midst of the stones of fire. Thy heart was lifted up because of thy beauty; thou hast corrupted thy wisdom by reason of thy brightness: I have cast thee to the ground; I have laid thee before kings, that they may behold thee. By the multitude of thine iniquities, in the unrighteousness of thy traffic, thou

hast profaned thy sanctuaries; therefore have I brought forth a fire from the midst of thee; it hath devoured thee, and I have turned thee to ashes upon the earth in the sight of all them that behold thee. All they that know thee among the peoples shall be astonished at thee: thou art become a terror, and thou shalt nevermore have any being.

God created Satan to become a cherub, one of the Almighty's most trusted and powerful servants. He fell because of his pride. He could not endure the beauty, the power, and the glory God had given him as the ruler of this world, and that is what caused him to turn against God—he wanted more, he wanted it all—he wanted the entire world and everything in it for himself. One factor that might have caused Satan to want to destroy Adam and take over his world is: when God gave Adam the entire creation as a gift of love—and Adam was lord of all—Satan was jealous.

Ezekiel's lamentation was pronounced against the king of Tyre, but the king of Tyre was not in Eden, nor was he a covering cherub. He had not been created to protect the holiness of God and oversee his new world; and none of what Ezekiel wrote applied to the king of Tyre. But Satan was in Eden, and he was a covering cherub. Satan had been created to oversee God's new world, and to work with God in assuring him that all was well throughout his entire empire—further evidence that all of this did apply to Satan! It is sad that Satan gave up such a glorious position in God's service as the overseer of his new world so he could establish his own power and authority by taking control of God's world for himself. He did that by tempting Adam and Eve to sin and turn the entire creation against God, thereby turning God against his own creation.

God did not destroy Satan when he sinned, for had he done so he would have had to destroy the whole creation with him, for it also had been defiled by sin (Romans 8:20). God did not strip

Satan of the power he had given him because he had sinned. He allowed him to continue as the prince of this world (John 12:31; 16:11), and as the god of this world (2 Corinthians 4:4), and as the prince of the powers of the air (Ephesians 2:1–2). If God had destroyed Satan and the creation with him, it would have been considered a failure for God to have created the world. But God does not tolerate failure, and he himself does not fail. Therefore, God annulled the sin Adam committed and abolished the consequences of his trespass by taking full responsibility for it himself. God paid in full for all the damage Adam's sin had caused with the blood of his only begotten Son. That allowed God to abolish sin and death in a holy and righteous way: The Almighty himself pleaded guilty to Adam's trespass; he suffered the guilt and the consequences of Adam's sin himself, and he paid in full for all the damage that Adam's trespass had caused with the cross of his only begotten Son. As a result of the cross Adam's sin—and all sin—was properly punished, and Adam and all sinners were forgiven and set free from sin and death—But! the sins men commit themselves are forgiven only when the sinner repents and accepts the forgiveness God offered them by obeying him, and keeping his commandments (John 8:31–32; Acts 2:38; 1 John 2:3, 3:24, 5:3). The impossible things God accomplished to save us from sin and death proves how much God loves us.

After Adam's trespass, instead of Satan working with God to protect his creation, and instead of there being peace and harmony between God and his new world—*there would be war!*

> And there was war in heaven: Michael and his angels going forth to war with the dragon; and the dragon warred and his angels; and they prevailed not, neither was their place found any more in heaven. And the great dragon was cast down, the old serpent, he that is called the Devil and Satan, the deceiver of the whole world; he was cast

down to the earth, and his angels were cast down with him. (Revelation 12:7-9).

God's battle was against Satan and all the angels who chose to rebel with him and defy the Almighty. It was those angels that became the demons, and they have no hope of restoration—not even through the cross (Hebrews 2:16). Their place would be in the pit of the abyss. Jude wrote, "And angels that kept not their own principality, but left their proper habitation, he hath kept in everlasting bonds under darkness unto the judgment of the great day" (Jude 1:6). Peter wrote, "For if God spared not angels when they sinned, but cast them down to hell, and committed them to pits of darkness, to be reserved unto judgment" (2 Peter 2:4). Satan also shall be cast into that dreaded place at the end of this present age when God judges the world, and that will be Satan's end—forever! (Revelation 20:2-3). That horrible place is called the lake of fire (Revelation 19:20, 20:10).

Next, God condemned the woman for her sin in eating of the fruit of the Tree of Knowledge and then tempting her husband to eat of it also. God told Eve that she would bear children in great pain and her husband would rule over her (Genesis 3:16; 1 Timothy 2:8–15). Such pain and such a relationship did not exist until after Eve had sinned and tempted Adam to follow her lead. That curse passed on to all generations of women after Eve, just ask any woman who has given birth to a baby. When women bring children into this world with great pain, they can thank Eve for causing that by her transgression.

Then God condemned the man, Adam, and he condemned the entire creation with him. Moses wrote in Genesis:

> And unto Adam he said, Because thou hast hear-
> kened unto the voice of thy wife, and hast eaten
> of the tree, of which I commanded thee, saying,
> Thou shalt not eat of it: cursed is the ground for

thy sake; in toil shalt thou eat of it all the days of thy life; thorns also and thistles shall it bring forth to thee; and thou shalt eat the herb of the field; in the sweat of thy face shalt thou eat bread, till thou return unto the ground; for out of it wast thou taken: for dust thou art, and unto dust shalt thou return. (Genesis 3:17–19)

What a price to pay for disobeying God's one simple commandment, "Stay away from my tree!" It was the moment Adam sinned that the entire creation was subjected to vanity, and farmers can thank Adam for the hard work it is to grow crops and face all the difficulties they experience in farming—and sometimes see nothing but failure in all of their hard work. Paul wrote:

For the earnest expectation of the creation waiteth for the revealing of the sons of God. For the creation was subjected to vanity, not of its own will, but by reason of him who subjected it, in hope that the creation itself also shall be delivered from the bondage of corruption into the liberty of the glory of the children of God. For we know that the whole creation groaneth and travaileth in pain together until now. (Romans 8:19–22)

Adam's trespass against God had horrible consequences. Not only was Adam sentenced to death because of his sin, but all humanity was sentenced to death with him, and the entre creation stood condemned because of his trespass. Paul wrote that the reason death passed on to all men when Adam sinned was because, when he sinned, all men sinned (Romans 5:12), and all men were made sinners by his transgression (Romans 5:19). That is not a statement many people (other than Catholics) will accept, but that is exactly what the verses in Romans 5:12–21 say. However, Jesus was the only man out of the entire human family who was made a sinner by Adam's trespass, and he was not only made a sinner—he was made to be sin. Paul wrote, "Him who knew no sin he made to be sin on our behalf; that we might become the righteousness of God in him" (2 Corinthians 5:21).

What a price Jesus was willing to pay to take the punishment we deserved upon himself and become our Savior—it is unimaginable. Paul wrote, "Therefore, as through one man sin entered into the world, and death through sin; and so death passed unto all men, for that all sinned" (Romans 5:12). "For as through the one man's disobedience the many were made sinners, even so through the obedience of the one shall the many be made righteous" (Romans 5:19). "For if, by the trespass of the one, death reigned through the one; much more shall they that receive the abundance of grace and of the gift of righteousness reign in life through the one, even Jesus Christ" (Romans 5:17). It is encouraging that in the same verse of Scripture that Paul said Adam's trespass made all men sinners and caused death to reign over them, he also said that the obedience of the One, who is Jesus, made all men righteous, ended the reign of death, and caused the reign of grace and life to rule over God's world, and all men. Both of those actions were simultaneous: Adam's sin immediately condemned the entire creation and passed a death sentence upon all men. However, in that same instant Jesus took that death sentence upon himself when he was willing to bear the guilt, the shame, and the entire consequence of Adam's transgression, and pay for it in full with the blood of his cross.

Jesus' Father accepted the sacrifice his Son offered to him from the cross as full compensation to restore all things back to their original perfection and beauty and take away the sins of the world (John 1:29)—and that included Adam's sin. However, there were other consequences of Adam's trespass that would not be corrected until the end of this present age, such as physical death and the continual deterioration of the entire universe.

It is called the second law of thermodynamics—entropy. While the theory of evolution teaches that everything is getting better, the facts continually declare that everything is falling apart and getting worse.

Death is the last enemy that shall be conquered by the cross of Jesus, and it is the last enemy of God that Jesus must face. Paul wrote:

> Then cometh the end, when he shall deliver up the kingdom to God, even the Father; when he shall have abolished all rule and all authority and power. For he must reign, till he hath put all his enemies under his feet. The last enemy that shall be abolished is death. (1 Corinthians 15:24–26)

Even physical death has already been conquered by Jesus' resurrection, and by the Father's promise of the general resurrection of all those who have died. Therefore—Christians do not die! When a Christian's life ends in this world, it is not death—their bodies just fall asleep, just as Steven's body "fell asleep" when he was stoned to death for preaching the Word (Acts 7:60). More often than not, when the Bible refers to the end of a Christian's life it is not referred to as death, it is called a sleep (1 Corinthians 15:6, 18, 20, 51; 1Thessolonians 4:13-18, 5:9-11). However, the moment that a person believes and obeys the Word of God, the gospel, and they are baptized, they enter a new world of eternal life where the sleep of death does not exist. John wrote, "Jesus said unto her, I am the resurrection, and the life: he that believeth on me, though he die, yet shall he live; and whosoever liveth and believeth on me shall never die. Believest thou this?" (John 11:25–26).

It was Adam's sin that brought death into the world and caused every living being to suffer death. However, Jesus' cross and his resurrection annihilated death and restored life to all. If there had been no cross then there could be no resurrection, and if there is no resurrection then there is no hope of life after death for anyone, and that includes sinless little babies. Paul wrote:

> Now if Christ is preached that he hath been raised from the dead, how say some among you that there is no resurrection of the dead? But if there is no resurrection of the dead, neither hath Christ been raised: and if Christ hath not been raised, then is our preaching vain, your faith also is vain. Yea, and we are found false witnesses of God; because we witnessed of God that he raised up Christ: whom he raised not up, if so be that the dead are not raised. For if the dead are not raised, neither hath Christ been raised: and if Christ hath not been raised, your faith is vain; ye are yet in your sins. Then they also that are fallen asleep in Christ have perished. If we have only hoped in Christ in this life, we are of all men most pitiable. But now hath Christ been raised from the dead, the firstfruits of them that are asleep. (1 Corinthians 15:13–19)

After Adam and Eve had broken God's law, and his heart, there were no more sins they could commit—because there was no other law for them to break. From the time of Adam to Moses there was no law, that is, no codified law such as the Law of Moses, and when there is no law there is no transgression of the law. Paul wrote, "For until the law sin was in the world; but sin is not imputed when there is no law" (Romans 5:13). "For as many as have sinned without law shall also perish without the law: and as many as have sinned under the law shall be judged by the law" (Romans 2:12). "For the law worketh wrath; but where there is no law, neither is there transgression" (Romans 4:15). That is why Paul wrote, "And the law came in besides, that the trespass might abound; but where sin abounded, grace did abound more exceedingly" (Romans 5:20). Moses' law was given to establish how evil and destructive sin is, establish the punishment required for every transgression, and the sacrifice necessary to forgive the sin.

There was no established law system from Adam to Moses, that is, a law stating what was right, what was wrong, and the punishment for breaking the law, *but there was law*. The law men were under from Adam to Moses was the law written in Romans 2:12-16:

> For as many as have sinned without law shall also perish without the law: and as many as have sinned under the law shall be judged by the law; for not the hearers of the law are just before God, but the doers of the law shall be justified: for when Gentiles that have not the law do by nature the things of the law, these, not having the law, are the law unto themselves; in that they show the work of the law written in their hearts, their conscience bearing witness therewith, and their thoughts one with another accusing or else excusing them; in the day when God shall judge the secrets of men, according to my gospel, by Jesus Christ.

When Adam sinned, he brought sin, death, and the knowledge of good and evil into the world, and those three things passed on to all men; but before Adam sinned, none of those things existed. Therefore, it was by the coming of the knowledge of good and evil that established the law for all men from the time of Adam to Moses, and it was the law for the Gentiles until the coming of the Christ.

Before Adam and Eve sinned they wore no clothes, they were naked, and they were not ashamed (Genesis 2:25). After they had eaten the forbidden fruit they were ashamed, for then they had the knowledge of good and evil. Immediately upon eating the fruit of the forbidden tree their eyes were opened and they knew they were naked, and they tried to make for themselves some clothing out of fig leaves (Genesis 3:7). God saw their sin, their problem, and how desperately they were trying to correct it, and so he made them clothing by killing an animal and using its skin to clothe them.

It was Adam's transgression that caused sin, death, and the knowledge of good and evil to enter the world, and into the minds of all men, and sin would occur when a person knew the right things to do and did not do them, or when they knew the wrong things that they should not do, and they did them anyway. But there was no *written law*, such as the Law of Moses to regulate what a person should or should not do, and no penalty had been established as the punishment for a transgression. Therefore, there was law, it was quite vague, but it was all men had to live by until Moses. Proof of this is, when the Gentiles did not have the law, but they did by nature (instinctively) the things of the law, they became the law unto themselves (Romans 2:14). Becoming the law unto themselves means there was law, and they were under that law.

With the coming of the knowledge of good and evil men intuitively knew right from wrong; they instinctively knew what was written in the Law of Moses; and that was because they had the knowledge of good and evil written in their minds and in their hearts. They had it written in their minds so they would know it, and it was written in their hearts so they would love it. Therefore, they were under law, and they were judged by how well they did not do the things they knew were wrong, and they did do what they knew to be right—and that was the law.

Proof that sins were imputed upon those who sinned be-tween the time from Adam to Moses is the flood: —*There was law*, because the entire creation was held accountable and pun-ished with death and destruction because of the terrible evil way people lived (Genesis 6:5-8).

The law for Israel was given to Moses when he was forty days and forty nights on Mount Sinai (Leviticus 26:46). That law was called The Ten Commandments, and there were some 613 other laws, all based on the Ten Commandments, which Israel was re-quired to keep. Therefore, between the time of Adam to Moses the only law that existed was the law of the knowledge of good and evil, *but that was law*, and when men did not keep it, they sinned.

When Moses received the Law for Israel, he perfectly re-ceived the instructions that declared how God wanted men to live, for the Law of Moses' perfectly and completely revealed the knowledge of good and evil (Galatians 3:24).

One day, about 1656 years after the creation, the entire world came to the point that all the people in it, except eight—the fam-ily of Noah—did not care about what they did, right or wrong; they lived evil lives, and they sinned. They trespassed against God by violating their consciences in such a dreadful way that God destroyed the entire world with a flood, and it was destroyed because of sin. Men were living evil lives because they did not care what was right or what was wrong; they just wanted to have a good time and live a life of ease and luxury that was pleasing to them. That is also why Sodom and Gomorrah were destroyed.

To show how vague the law was between Adam and Moses, we should view the murder of Abel by his brother Cain. Cain and Abel were Adam's and Eve's first children. Cain became very upset with his brother Abel, and it was all caused by how they worshipped God. Abel was very careful to do all things correct-ly, and God had great respect for Abel and his offering. But Cain just threw some things together and he did what was easy. As a result, God reprimanded him. Cain did not take that lightly, and it caused him such contempt for God and his brother that he murdered Abel. Moses wrote about all that in Genesis 4:3–16.

When Cain murdered his brother, he knew he had done wrong, and God also knew he had done wrong (Genesis 4:8-16), even though there was no law that said, "Thou shalt not kill." They instinctively knew murder was wrong! Under the Law of Moses Cain would have been executed by stoning (Exodus 21:14–15). But instead of Cain being punished with death for his transgression, he was driven from the land he lived in, and God protected him from the death sentence he knew he deserved. That is something that is very difficult to understand.

When Adam sinned, it caused death to reign over all men because of his trespass. Death also ruled over men because of their own sins, even though they had not sinned after the likeness of Adam's transgression. Adam sinned by breaking the one law he was required to keep. There were other men who sinned after Adam had trespassed, but they did not sin after the likeness of Adam's transgression—Adam sinned by breaking the law, but other men could not sin by breaking the law because there was no law for them to break—they sinned by violating their conscience, or by violating their knowledge of the law of good and evil. That *law* required a person to do what was right and not do what was wrong according to their knowledge of good and evil. Therefore, men sinned by doing wrong when they knew they were doing wrong, and they did not care. Even when a person does something they think is wrong, but it is not wrong, they have sinned because it was not done in faith (Romans 14:23). For instance, Paul said that eating meat that had been sacrificed to idols was not a sin. However, if the person eating it thought it was a sin, and they ate it anyway, then to them it was sin (Romans 14:14-23; 1 Corinthians 8:1-13).

The people who lived without law were the people who lived in the time of ignorance when their sins were *overlooked* (Acts

17:30). That time ended with the coming of the Christ. When there was no written law men were ignorant of what God required of them—and that was the time of ignorance. Luke wrote, "The times of ignorance therefore God overlooked; but now he commandeth men that they should all everywhere repent: inasmuch as he hath appointed a day in which he will judge the world in righteousness by the man whom he hath ordained; whereof he hath given assurance unto all men, in that he hath raised him from the dead" (Acts 17:30–31). Therefore, their sins were *overlooked,* but they did not just vanish and go away; their sins were punished and paid for in full by being nailed to the cross of Jesus. The times of ignorance ended for the Jews when Moses received the Law. It ended for the Gentiles and all men on the day of the cross. That was the day when it was required that all men must believe in Jesus, the Son of God, and that he had died on the cross to forgive all men of all sin (Acts 17:30-31). When Jesus came and ended the time of ignorance it became necessary to believe the Word of God and abide in that Word (John 8:31–32), and that requires knowledge (Hosea 4:6, Romans 10:2).

The Gentiles had always lived without written law from the time of Adam to the time of Christ, for the Gentiles were never under the Law of Moses (Psalms 147:19–20), and there was no other law that God had given them. Therefore, God destroyed Sodom and Gomorrah with fire, and he destroyed the ancient world with a flood at a time when there was no law. The men in both times did not care about how they lived, or how many times they defiled their consciences, and that is why they were destroyed. Maybe they had become so bold that they no longer had a conscience. They just lived according to their own passions and pleasures and did what was pleasing to them, according to what was delightful in their own eyes (Judges 21:25).

People escape all of that when they become Christians by believing in Jesus; that he is the Son of God, and that he was crucified and raised from the dead to forgive all sinners (John

8:24, Romans 10:9). Then, when they are baptized all their sins are washed away by the blood of Christ (Acts 22:16) and at that point they have a pure and clean conscience void of offence (Hebrews 9:14). But what happens when a person sins after they are baptized? They remain sinless by living a Christian life, and that is accomplished by abiding in the truth according to Jesus' commandments (John 8:31–32; 1 John 2:3–5); and by walking in the light (1 John 1:7); and the light Christians walk in is Almighty God himself (1 John 1:5). Anyone who lives such a life will never be charged with sin (1 John 3:9), because they are immediately forgiven.

Conscience is a powerful tool, and when it is correctly programmed according to the will of God, according to the knowledge of good and evil, and it is obeyed; it can keep one from sin. But a person's conscience alone is not law. Law is a system of rules and regulations that must be obeyed, and when those laws are broken that same law system determines the punishment that must be administered for each transgression. Also, there are some things that are wrong no matter what a person's conscience thinks about them; such things as murder, stealing, adultery, lying, and other evil actions of one person against another that cause grievous harm. Those deeds are confirmed to be evil just by the action it takes to commit them, as well as the horrible consequences that result from them.

To sum this all up in a few words: it was one man and his evil act of disobedience that brought sin and death into the world, sentenced the entire creation to annihilation, and pronounced the death sentence against all living beings. His name was Adam, and he was the first son of God (Luke 3:38). It was another Man whose name is Jesus, he was Adam's brother, and he is the only begotten Son of God (John 3:16-28). He annulled his brother's sin and abolished its consequences by his cross and his resurrection. Jesus abolished spiritual death with his cross when he cried, "Eli, Eli, lama sabachthani? that is, My God, my God, why hast thou forsaken me?" (Matthew 27:46). That was the moment when Jesus drank the cup that he so feverishly prayed in the garden he would not have to drink (Matthew 26:39–44), and that was the moment his spirit died (Isaiah 53:12). That was the moment when he was separated from God to take away the sins of the world. It was that moment when Jesus became sin, and so when he died, sin died (2 Corinthians 5:21). That is also the moment Jesus became the curse for sin, and when he died, the curse for sin died with him (Galatians 3:13). The curse of sin is death. It was Jesus who took that curse upon himself when he paid in full for all the damage that Adam's sin had caused. That was the moment Jesus abolished the reign of death that was pronounced against all men, and he established the reign of life (Romans 5:17). The reign of death has ended, and the reign of life has been established for all those who believe in and obey Jesus. However, the actual restoration of all things has not yet transpired (Acts 3:19-21), but that will take place when Jesus coms again and this old world is annihilated by fire and the new heavens and the new earth wherein dwells righteousness shall forever be established as the eternal dwelling place for all of God's children (2 Peter 3:7-13). What a wonderful blessing and privilege it is for Christians to be in heaven with God and behold the passing away of this present evil world when Jesus comes again. Then! We shall witness the building and the establishment of the new heavens and the new earth wherein dwelleth righteousness (2 Peter 3:13). And that will be our home forever!

CHAPTER 3

WHY DID THE SIN OF ONE MAN CONDEMN THE ENTIRE CREATION AND SENTENCE ALL MEN TO DEATH?

WHEN TRYING TO COMPREHEND why God would condemn his entire creation and pass the death sentence upon the entire world of all living beings for the sin of just one man, Adam, we must understand who Adam was, what Adam had been given, and what he did that was so severe that it caused God to take such drastic action. It was Adam's trespass that forced all men and even the animals to be faced with death (Hebrews 9:27–28)—but why? Before Adam sinned, there was no such thing as sin or death. It must have been a very evil thing that Adam did to cause such a mighty and terrifying destructive force as death to come into God's perfect world and threaten to kill all men. There were other sins that other men had committed that to us seem to be much more serious than what Adam did. When David sinned by committing adultery with another man's wife, Bathsheba, and then had her husband murdered to cover up his crime (2 Samuel

11:1–17), he committed two capital crimes that were not for-givable under the Old Law (Leviticus 20:10; Numbers 35:15–21, 30-32). But David was forgiven the very moment he confessed his sin and repented (2 Samuel 12:13). However, David suffered severe consequences for the rest of his life for the terrible sin he had committed (2 Samuel 12:7–12). Likewise, Adam and Eve were forgiven for their trespass, if they accepted God's forgive-ness, but the abiding consequences of their sin remain in this present evil world to this day: death, and the continual deterio-ration of the world God created. Those evil forces shall remain in the world until Jesus comes again.

David never offered a sacrifice, or a sin-offering for the trans-gressions he committed. But when he confessed his sins he was forgiven instantly for the two sins he had arrogantly carried out. The reason David never offered a sin-offering is because accord-ing to the Law there was no sacrifice that could be offered to for-give either of his sins. They were both capital crimes demanding the death of the transgressor. But David was forgiven anyway, and he was called a man after God's own heart (1 Samuel 13:14; Acts 13:22). The reason David received such merciful forgive-ness was because of his lifestyle from the time he was a shepherd boy until he became the king of Israel. When David was strug-gling every moment of his life just to stay alive, he always asked God for his advice and his help. However, when David became the king he could not bear the glory of such success. So also it was with his son, Solomon (1 Kings 11:4-6). It was David's na-ture to be faithful to God and to trust the Almighty with all his heart and soul when that was necessary every moment of his life just to stay alive. But when all was well, and David was bored, things changed. This is a warning to all to not become boast-ful and proud, in an arrogant way, when God blesses them with great success, and they think, "I have arrived!"

So, when David had committed such a grave act of immoral disobedience that could not be forgiven under the Old Covenant, why was there declared such a drastic penalty against Adam for such a simple act of disobedience as eating a piece of fruit from a forbidden tree? There is a very reasonable answer to that question. When Adam sinned, sin and death did not exist in God's new world. It was Adam who brought sin and death into the world, and because of that the penalty for such an act of disobedience was infinitely severe—it had to be that way because this was the first sin, and the punishment it demanded set the standard for the punishment of all other sins of like manner—breaking God's law. The sins that would be committed many times by many men must be punished in a just manner, and it was Adam's transgression that set the standard for that punishment. By Adam's one act of disobedience, he condemned everything God created. But when David sinned he was just one sinner among many. David sinned when God dealt with each man's trespass according to what he had done, according to the Law, and according to his grace and mercy. The penalty for the sins that men committed under the Law did not affect anyone but the person who had committed them. Each man was punished only for his own sin (Ezekiel 18:4, 20). But the consequence of Adam's trespass affected the entire creation and every living being in it.

Adam was the son of God (Luke 3:38), and he had been created in the image of God (Genesis 1:26–27). As God's son he had been given dominion over the entire creation and everything in it (Genesis 1:26–28). Adam lacked nothing, and nothing more could be given to him except the one thing that was forbidden: the Tree of the Knowledge of Good and Evil. Adam did not need that tree; in fact, it was a detriment for him to have it. Without the Tree of the Knowledge of Good and Evil Adam and Eve were innocent. They had no knowledge of good or evil, and therefore they had only one law to keep—and that made life very simple. All they had to do was to live day by day, to enjoy life, and "to dress and to keep the garden"—which gave them something to do (Genesis 2:15). They were also to have children and repopulate the world as God had commanded them (Genesis 1:28). That would give them plenty to do. At that time there was no pain involved for a woman when she gave birth to a child (Genesis 3:16). What more could they want? However, that tree was a severe temptation because it was in the midst of the Garden, it was beautiful (Genesis 2:9), and it had been forbidden upon the penalty of death for the transgression of partaking of its fruit—That tree was holy—It belonged to God! Moses wrote:

> And Jehovah God commanded the man, saying, Of every tree of the garden thou mayest freely eat: but of the tree of the knowledge of good and evil, thou shalt not eat of it: for in the day that thou eatest thereof thou shalt surely die. (Genesis 2:16–17)

With all that Adam and Eve had been given, it was still not enough—they wanted more, and they were going to take it. That is why their transgression against the Almighty was so severe. They were God's beloved children who had been given life in the image of their Father, God, they had been given everything their Father had created, and they violated the one and only law their Father had given them. That is the reason Adam brought two mighty and terrifying evil forces into the world—evil forces that did not exist until he initiated them by sinning—they were the evil forces of sin and death.

It was not Adam who first ate of the fruit of the Tree of Knowledge, it was Eve. It was the serpent who deceived Eve and tempted her to violate the one commandment God had given them. Adam and Eve were probably quite familiar with the serpent, as they all lived in the garden together. They probably saw it often. Therefore, when the serpent approached Eve, not Adam, she was most likely not startled at all, for the serpent was just another friendly acquaintance. Moses wrote about all of that and exactly what happened that caused the fall of the entire creation in Genesis 3:1–24. It would be advisable to read that chapter now to see exactly what happened.

By Moses' account we can see that Eve was standing by the Tree of Knowledge and admiring its beauty. Satan was waiting for that opportunity; for he knew that at that moment she was quite vulnerable. She saw that the tree was good for food, pleasant to the eyes, and "to be desired to make one wise" (Genesis 3:6). Those are the three temptations that John said could trap any person into sin, and one must be very careful to avoid them, when he wrote:

> Love not the world, neither the things that are in the world. If any man love the world, the love of the Father is not in him. For all that is in the world, the lust of the flesh and the lust of the eyes and the vain glory of life, is not of the Father, but is of the world. And the world passeth away, and the lust thereof: but he that doeth the will of God abideth for ever (1 John 2:15–17).

Adam was standing right there with Eve when the devil tempted her, but he did nothing to interfere. He allowed her to eat the fruit of the tree, and then she gave the fruit of the tree to Adam. He also ate it (Genesis 3:6), and that is what made Adam responsible for all that happened that day. Eve was deceived, and that is why she sinned. But Adam was not deceived. When Adam ate the fruit of the forbidden tree, he knew full well what he was doing and that he was violating the one commandment of God that he had been given. Paul wrote, "For Adam was first formed, then Eve; and Adam was not beguiled, but the woman being beguiled hath fallen into transgression" (1 Timothy 2:13–14). Why did Adam commit such an evil act of disobedience when he knew it was so very wrong? Only God knows the answer to that question, but that was why Adam was held accountable for what happened—he was the one to whom the commandment not to eat of the tree had been given (Genesis 2:16–17), he was the one who allowed it to happen, and he ate of the fruit of the forbidden tree anyway. One thing that needs to be mentioned here is that the Tree of Life has been restored, and it is freely offered to every person who desires to eat of it and have eternal life. It is called the Cross of Jesus (Revelation 2:7; 22:2, 14).

Paul wrote Romans 5:12–21 to give an answer to two questions: Why did God condemn the entire creation and sentence all living beings in it to death for the sin of one man? And what would be necessary to annul Adam's trespass and restore the creation back to its original glory and perfection, reinstating life to Adam and to all who had perished because of his sin? For all of that to be accomplished it would require something extremely powerful and extraordinary. A ransom must be paid that was of such infinite value that its magnitude was inconceivable (Matthew 20:28; 1 Timothy 2:5–6). That ransom required that God himself must leave his Holy Place and become a Man. He would be called Immanuel, the Messiah, the Christ, the Son of man and the Son of God. He would become God's only begotten Son, and he came into this world for the express purpose of being spit on, humiliated, beaten, crowned with thorns, and nailed to a cross to be lifted up on the cross and left to die.

When Jesus annulled the consequence of Adam's trespass by the power of his cross, he restored the world that Adam's sin had destroyed back into its original beauty, glory, and perfection. That new world is called the kingdom of God. It is a spiritual world. It is the world Christians live in, which is the church (Matthew 16:18; Hebrews 12:22–24). It is possible that the new world Christians shall live in when this age ends (when the new heavens and the new earth are established) will be much better than the world Adam and Eve lived in even before their world was condemned by Adam's trespass. The new heavens and the new earth that are yet to come shall be perfectly spiritual, and they shall be continually protected forever from sin and death by the blood of Christ. Peter wrote:

> But the day of the Lord will come as a thief; in the which the heavens shall pass away with a great noise, and the elements shall be dissolved with fervent heat, and the earth and the works that are therein shall be burned up. Seeing that these things are thus all to be dissolved, what manner of persons ought ye to be in all holy living and godliness, looking for and earnestly desiring the coming of the day of God, by reason of which the heavens being on fire shall be dissolved, and the elements shall melt with fervent heat? But, according to his promise, we look for new heavens and a new earth, wherein dwelleth righteousness. Wherefore, beloved, seeing that ye look for these things, give diligence that ye may be found in peace, without spot and blameless in his sight. (2 Peter 3:10–14)

We know that the new heavens and the new earth shall be a spiritual world because that is the world where God's children shall live with their Father forever. God is Spirit (John 4:24) and when God's children are resurrected, and their bodies are once again given new life, their new bodies shall be spiritual bodies. Paul wrote:

> So also is the resurrection of the dead. It is sown in corruption; it is raised in incorruption: it is sown in dishonor; it is raised in glory: it is sown in weakness; it is raised in power: it is sown a natural body; it is raised a spiritual body. If there is

a natural body, there is also a spiritual body. (1 Corinthians 15:42–44)

Spiritual people with spiritual bodies can only live in a spiritual world because flesh and blood cannot inherit the kingdom of God (1 Corinthians 15:50). The new heavens and the new earth are the new spiritual world where the children of God shall live with their Father forever. Since God is Spirit (John 4:24) and his children shall be spiritual, they shall all be just like their Father, who is God (1 John 3:1–3).

Adam and Eve sinned by breaking the only law God had given them. However, there were two other commandments that were not truly laws. Adam and Eve were to stay in the garden and "dress it and keep it" (Genesis 2:15), and they were to have children and replenish the world with their own kind (Genesis 1:27–28). There was no penalty mentioned for breaking either one of those commandments, and therefore they were not truly laws. Any true law system must state very clearly what a person must do, what they must not do, and the penalty for disobedience. The Law of Moses did that perfectly. Therefore, there was no other way Adam and Eve could have trespassed against God other than by breaking the one commandment God had given them, not to eat the fruit of the Tree of the Knowledge of Good and Evil (Genesis 2:16–17).

That tree was in the midst of the garden where it could be seen and admired by Adam and Eve every day, and it was very beautiful. The Tree of Life was also in the midst of the garden, but Adam had not been forbidden to eat of the fruit of that tree (Genesis 2:9.)

This causes a person to wonder why God made the forbidden tree when he knew it would be such a severe temptation to Adam and Eve; and he knew that they would ultimately eat of it and sin. God also knew that they would condemn everything he had made by their disobedience—including themselves. However, without that tree, and without God's commandment to not eat of it, which required obedience, respect, and love, there would have been no other way for God's children to have demonstrated their loyalty, their love, and their respect for their Father and his will. God did not want puppets on a string, or robots that that had no mind of their own and could do nothing else but exactly what they were programed to do. He wanted children who would love him, reverence him, and obey him by their own volition because they respected him and loved him above everything else. All God wants from us is for us to believe him, obey him, and love him; when Abraham did that he was reckoned righteous, and he was called the friend of God (Galatians 3:6; James 2:20-23).

Why would it be considered such a severe crime for such a simple act of disobedience that caused the condemnation of God's entire creation? The answer to that question is—it was no simple act of disobedience! It was brazen! Adam and Eve had a direct command from God as to what was forbidden, and they knew the penalty for disobedience—Death! They knew they were required to obey that command of their own free will. For Adam and Eve to be well-pleasing to their Father they must choose to subject themselves to his will and his commands by their own volition. But they did not do that. They went against God and his Word by dishonoring his one simple command—and they sinned! Their sin was caused by a lack of respect and love for their Father who had given them life and everything he had—his entire creation.

But why did God hold his entire creation accountable for one man's sin? (Romans 8:19–22). Why did God pass a death sentence upon the entire human race for the sin of just one man? (Romans 5:12–17; 1 Corinthians 15:21–22; Hebrews 9:27–28). When we examine the six days of the creation, and the marvelous blessings that God had given to Adam on the very day he was given life, we can better understand why all things were condemned by his sin. Everything in the new world belonged to Adam. God had appointed him as the lord over it all (Genesis 1:26–28). It is possible that appointment might have been a real problem for Satan, for he also was the prince of this world (John 12:31, 16:11), the prince of the powers of the air (Ephesians 2:2), and the god of this world (2 Corinthians 4:4). It is possible there might have been a little jealousy there, and that could be one of the reasons Satan tempted Eve to eat the forbidden fruit. Satan was going to determine once and for all who truly was the master of God's new creation, and if Adam was charged with sin, it certainly would not be him. Therefore, when Adam sinned and stood condemned, everything he owned stood condemned with him. Adam's entire family, (that is, his family that had yet to come into the world and populate the world—the human family) also stood condemned with him—but why? God considered Adam and Eve and the world in which they lived to be just one united entity. Therefore, when any part of it was contaminated, it all became corrupt. What Adam did to the Almighty was a terrible blow to him, for it grieved God greatly to have to pass a death sentence upon his own precious children (Genesis 6:5–7) and to have to condemn his entire creation with them (Romans 8:19–23).

In the Old Testament if a man sinned against God by violating something that God owned—that is, something that was holy unto God—it was not uncommon for the Almighty to hold the man, his entire family, and everything the man possessed accountable for his trespass. Therefore, the man, his family, and all of his possessions would stand condemned with him because of his sin, and when that man was punished for his crime his entire family and everything he owned was reprimanded with him. There was an instance when that happened as it is recorded in the Bible. When Israel conquered Jericho, they had conquered the first and the mightiest city in their new promised land. Therefore, that city was holy. It was devoted to the Almighty, and everything in that city belonged to God. No man was to take anything out of that city to be his own private possession upon the pain of death. Joshua wrote:

> And it came to pass at the seventh time, when the priests blew the trumpets, Joshua said unto the people, Shout; for Jehovah hath given you the city. And the city shall be devoted, even it and all that is therein, to Jehovah: only Rahab the harlot shall live, she and all that are with her in the house, because she hid the messengers that we sent. But as for you, only keep yourselves from the devoted thing, lest when ye have devoted it, ye take of the devoted thing; so would ye make the camp of Israel accursed, and trouble it. But all the silver, and gold, and vessels of brass and iron, are holy unto Jehovah: they shall come into the treasury of Jehovah. (Joshua 6:16–19)

Joshua told the Israelites that Jericho, the city they were about to take was devoted to the Almighty, and everything in the city was holy unto God and belonged to God. If any Israelite took something from that city to be their own possession, then they were stealing from God, and the guilt for their trespass would fall upon the whole nation of Israel. They were also robbing the brotherhood of all Israel! (Joshua 6:19). But there was a greedy man named Achan who was willing to take the risk and steal from God (and Israel). When Achan stole some silver and gold and a beautiful Babylonian mantle from the devoted city and hid them in his tent (Joshua 7:21), all the nation of Israel was held accountable for his trespass. Joshua wrote, "But the children of Israel committed a trespass in the devoted thing; for Achan, the son of Carmi, the son of Zabdi, the son of Zerah, of the tribe of

Judah, took of the devoted thing: and the anger of Jehovah was kindled against the children of Israel" (Joshua 7:1).

When Achan stole some valuables from Jericho, it was the whole nation of Israel that God held accountable for his trespass. Therefore, the whole nation of Israel became the object of God's wrath, not just Achan. When Achan stole his treasure from God, the Almighty did not say to Joshua that Achan had sinned, he said, "Israel hath sinned!" (Joshua 7:11). It was because of Achan's trespass that God's anger was kindled against all the children of Israel (Joshua 7:1). As a result of Achan's trespass Israel could not conquer even the least one of the cities of the Promised Land, and in an attempt to take a very small city called Ai, many Israelites died (Joshua 7:2–6) —and they died because of Achan's sin! God was angry with the whole nation of Israel, and he would no longer aid the nation in any way until the problem Achan created had been recognized, solved, and corrected (Joshua 7:2–9). Joshua wrote:

> Israel hath sinned; yea, they have even transgressed my covenant which I commanded them: yea, they have even taken of the devoted thing, and have also stolen, and dissembled also; and they have even put it among their own stuff. Therefore the children of Israel cannot stand before their enemies; they turn their backs before their enemies, because they are become accursed: I will not be with you any more, except ye destroy the devoted thing from among you. (Joshua 7:11–12)

To correct the problem Achan caused, Joshua called the entire nation of Israel before him, and by drawing lots the guilt fell upon Achan (Joshua 7:14–19). Achan confessed his sin, and it did not go well for that man or for his family. Joshua wrote:

And Achan answered Joshua, and said, Of a truth I have sinned against Jehovah, the God of Israel, and thus and thus have I done: when I saw among the spoil a goodly Babylonish mantle, and two hundred shekels of silver, and a wedge of gold of fifty shekels weight, then I coveted them, and took them; and, behold, they are hid in the earth in the midst of my tent, and the silver under it. (Joshua 7:20–21)

It is interesting that the crime Achan committed was a capital crime, and there was no sacrifice that could be offered to forgive Achan and his family for their sin. The penalty for their transgression was death, and there was no way to escape that fate. Therefore, the sentence of death was declared against Achan, his wife, his children, his animals, and everything he owned. They were all taken out to a place called the valley of Achor and executed by being stoned to death and then burned. The valley of Achor is "the valley of trouble." It was so named because of Achan's trespass and execution. Joshua wrote:

And Joshua, and all Israel with him, took Achan the son of Zerah, and the silver, and the mantle, and the wedge of gold, and his sons, and his daughters, and his oxen, and his asses, and his sheep, and his tent, and all that he had: and they brought them up unto the valley of Achor. And Joshua said, Why hast thou troubled us? Jehovah shall trouble thee this day. And all Israel stoned him with stones; and they burned them with fire, and stoned them with stones. And they raised over him a great heap of stones, unto this day; and Jehovah turned from the fierceness of his anger.

> Wherefore the name of that place was called, The
> valley of Achor, unto this day. (Joshua 7:24–26)

Achan was just the common head of a small Israelite family.
But Achan was an Israelite, and when he violated something that
was holy unto God, all the children of Israel were held accountable for his trespass. When we view what a serious act of disobedience it was for Achan to steal from God by robbing him of his
devoted things, and we see the punishment that fell upon him,
his family, and everything he owned because of his transgression, we can better understand why God condemned the entire
creation for what Adam had done. Adam had done exactly the
same thing Achan did—he stole from God. Adam was not just
a member of the human family; he was the head of the human
family. Adam was not just part of the creation; he was the master
of the creation. That is why when Adam was condemned for his
trespass the entire creation and all humanity were held accountable and condemned with him.

By Achan's sin, and Adam's trespass, we can better understand how deadly it is to disregard something that is holy unto
God as just common and ordinary and fail to honor it the way
God honors it. That is why our church participation (praying,
singing, and giving) should be carried out with the greatest care
and respect for God that is possible. The Lord's Supper is most
holy because it is a remembrance that offers participation in the
cross and suffering of our Savior. To not honor that holiness
with the highest reverence is something God will not tolerate.
Likewise, the name of God is most holy, and it should never be
used in a common or vulgar way (Exodus 20:7). When people
today are not careful in their service, their giving, and their wor-
ship of their Father, and his Son, God considers that robbery.
Malachi wrote:

Will a man rob God? yet ye rob me. But ye say, Wherein have we robbed thee? In tithes and offerings. Ye are cursed with the curse; for ye rob me, even this whole nation. Bring ye the whole tithe into the store-house, that there may be food in my house, and prove me now herewith, saith Jehovah of hosts, if I will not open you the windows of heaven, and pour you out a blessing, that there shall not be room enough to receive it. (Malachi 3:8-10)

The reason Adam's trespass was so very serious is because he had been given life in the very image of God his Father, and God was his only Father. Adam truly was the son of God (Luke 3:38). That is what made Adam and Jesus brothers. They were each one a son of God, and the Almighty was their only Father. They each one did something that affected the entire creation and everything in it: Adam sinned and condemned it—Jesus' righteous act of obedience on the cross saved it. That is what made Adam a figure, or a type of Christ, the one who was to come (Romans 5:14).

Everything God created in the heavens and upon the earth and in the sea were all given to Adam, and he had dominion over them all. Genesis 1:26–27 says:

And God said, Let us make man in our image, after our likeness: and let them have dominion over the fish of the sea, and over the birds of the heavens, and over the cattle, and over all the earth, and over every creeping thing that creepeth upon the earth. And God created man in his own image, in the image of God created he him; male and female created he them.

However, Jesus, Adam's brother, was given all authority over all things in heaven and on earth just before he ascended into the heavens as a reward for his work of redemption. Matthew 28:18–20 says:

> And Jesus came to them and spake unto them, saying, All authority hath been given unto me in heaven and on earth. Go ye therefore, and make disciples of all the nations, baptizing them into the name of the Father and of the Son and of the Holy Spirit: teaching them to observe all things whatsoever I commanded you: and lo, I am with you always, even unto the end of the world.

God gave Adam, his son, dominion over the entire creation on the very day he was created (Genesis 1:26–27). He was given such a great gift because of God's love for him. But Adam lost everything he had been given because of his disobedience and disrespect for his Father. Jesus, the only begotten Son of God was given everything Adam lost, and it was all given to him because of the love and respect that Jesus had for his Father, as well as his righteous and holy obedience.

Adam's spirit was created in the image of God—not his physical body that could die and decay. Hebrews 12:9 says, "Furthermore, we had the fathers of our flesh to chasten us, and we gave them reverence: shall we not much rather be in subjection unto the Father of spirits, and live?" Even the animals have spirits that keep their bodies alive, and when their spirits leave their bodies they die, just like humans die. Ecclesiastics 3:18–21 says:

> I said in my heart, It is because of the sons of men, that God may prove them, and that they may see that they themselves are but as beasts. For that

which befalleth the sons of men befalleth beasts;
even one thing befalleth them: as the one dieth,
so dieth the other; yea, they have all one breath;
and man hath no preeminence above the beasts:
for all is vanity. All go unto one place; all are of
the dust, and all turn to dust again. Who knoweth
the spirit of man, whether it goeth upward, and
the spirit of the beast, whether it goeth down-
ward to the earth?

This causes a person to wonder—what happens to animals when they die? What happens to their spirits? If Solomon did not know, then we certainly do not know either. I have always been bothered by the thought of how animals must suffer and die because of one man's sin when they themselves have never sinned. However, God is just, righteous, and holy, and he will not do anything, or tolerate anything that is questionable. The common view of most men is that when animals die they just disappear as if they had never existed. Maybe that is true—or is it? Animals have never sinned against God, and God loves them dearly. Matthew wrote, "Are not two sparrows sold for a penny? and not one of them shall fall on the ground without your Father (Matthew 10:29). Luke wrote, "Are not five sparrows sold for two pence? and not one of them is forgotten in the sight of God" (Luke 12:6). Yet, when animals die, they die because of Adam's sin. Just as all men must die and their bodies return to dust (Genesis 3:19) —all which was caused by the sin of one man, Adam—so also it is with the animals. Will the spirits of the animals be found in heaven with the spirits and the resurrected bodies of the children of God who have obeyed him? Solomon, the wisest man who ever lived (1 Kings 3:1–12), said he did not know (Ecclesiastics 3:18–21). But if they are in heaven, then the new world of the Christians will be exactly like it was when God originally created it in the beginning and gave it all to Adam—it

99

will be full of all kinds of living creatures, and since heaven is a very big place, and since God loves life, I believe the above is a very reasonable conclusion. Luke wrote:

> Repent ye therefore, and turn again, that your sins may be blotted out, that so there may come seasons of refreshing from the presence of the Lord; and that he may send the Christ who hath been appointed for you, even Jesus: whom the heaven must receive until the times of restoration of all things, whereof God spake by the mouth of His holy prophets that have been from of old. (Acts 3:19–21)

The restoration *"of all things"* means—*all things.* That would include the animal world and everything else in the world that had been created by the Almighty but had been defiled by Adam's sin.

Just as God gave Adam dominion over the original creation (Genesis 1:26), so also the children of God shall have dominion over the new heavens and the new earth (that is, the new creation, the kingdom of God), which includes the world that is yet to come. Luke wrote, "Fear not, little flock; for it is your Father's good pleasure to give you the kingdom" (Luke 12:32). That kingdom is the new world of God (the church), and it belongs to the saints because God gave it to them. In the church Christians own everything God created, and they own it in conjunction with God and his Son, Jesus. God has made Christians equal heirs with his only begotten Son. The writer of the Hebrew letter had this to say:

> God, having of old time spoken unto the fathers in the prophets by divers portions and in divers manners, hath at the end of these days spoken

unto us in his Son, whom he appointed heir of all things, through whom also he made the worlds. (Hebrews 1:1–2)

This scripture says that Jesus inherited everything that belonged to God, His Father and our Father, His God and our God (John 20:17); and that includes his kingdom. Paul wrote in the Roman letter:

For as many as are led by the Spirit of God, these are sons of God. For ye received not the spirit of bondage again unto fear; but ye received the spirit of adoption, whereby we cry, Abba, Father. The Spirit himself beareth witness with our spirit, that we are children of God; and if children, then heirs; heirs of God, and joint-heirs with Christ; if so be that we suffer with him, that we may be also glorified with him. (Romans 8:14–17)

Every Christian shall inherit equally from the Father all the things Jesus inherited, and he inherited everything. When all of that transpires God will have exactly what he wanted when he created the world of Adam and Eve. It is because of God's love that he wants his children to own everything he made for them, and to richly enjoy all the good things he has given them to enjoy (1 Timothy 6:17). God created the world so his children, Adam and Eve, would have a perfect place to live, and so he would have something very valuable to give to them as a precious gift. This will also be the case with the new creation. Christians shall own the kingdom of God and everything in it equally with Christ. God's children shall not be ruled over by the Christ, they will rule with him. Paul wrote, "Faithful is the saying: For if we died with him, we shall also live with him: if we endure, we shall also reign with him: if we shall deny him, he also will deny us" (2 Timothy 2:11–12).

Let us view a few of the reasons that God's creation and his children were so perfect, so holy, and so precious to the Almighty—and why God demanded that everything must remain that way for his new world to endure.

First, the creation did not just happen. It has not always been in existence, and it did not just suddenly appear. It took God six days for him to create his new world, and those six days were such days as we know in our present time. To view it any other way denies the power of God. At the end of each day God admired what he had created, just as a master carpenter views his masterpiece that he has finished. God rejoiced in his work, for it was perfect and beautiful. There was not one flaw in any part of what he had made. After viewing each of his day's work, God said, "it is good!" On the final day, the sixth day, God viewed everything he had made, and he said, "It is very good!" (Genesis 1:31).

The creation had been in the mind of God forever, and when the proper time came he fulfilled his thoughts and made them real by speaking them into existence. Revelation 4:11 says, "Worthy art thou, our Lord and our God, to receive the glory and the honor and the power: for thou didst create all things, and because of thy will they were, and were created." The things of the creation *"were"* when they were forever in the mind of God, and they *"were created"* when the time came that he spoke them into their existence and made them real. It was God the Father who designed the creation and spoke it into its existence (Psalms 148:1-5). It was the Word of God, who is God (John 1:1-2), who took what the Father had designed and spoken, and he physically created space, mass (or matter), energy, and time (Genesis 1:1–5). John wrote:

In the beginning was the Word, and the Word was with God, and the Word was God. The same was in the beginning with God. All things were made through him; and without him was not anything made that hath been made. In him was life; and the life was the light of men. (John 1:1–4)

Hebrews 1:1–2 says:

God, having of old time spoken unto the fathers in the prophets by divers portions and in divers manners, hath at the end of these days spoken unto us in his Son, whom he appointed heir of all things, through whom also he made the worlds.

Paul wrote:

Giving thanks unto the Father, who made us meet to be partakers of the inheritance of the saints in light; who delivered us out of the power of darkness, and translated us into the kingdom of the Son of his love; in whom we have our redemption, the forgiveness of our sins: who is the image of the invisible God, the firstborn of all creation; for in him were all things created, in the heavens and upon the earth, things visible and things invisible, whether thrones or dominions or principalities or powers; all things have been created through him, and unto him; and he is before all things, and in him all things consist [hold together]. And he is the head of the body, the church: who is the beginning, the firstborn from the dead; that in all things he might have the preeminence. (Colossians 1:12–18)

But what the Word created had no organization—it was nothing short of disarray. Moses wrote, "And the earth was waste and void; and darkness was upon the face of the deep: and the Spirit of God moved upon the face of the waters" (Genesis 1:2). It was the Holy Spirit who vibrated (or "moved") over the waters and organized everything the Word had created, and he fashioned it into the perfectly organized, predictable, orderly, and beautiful world we live in today (Genesis 1:2). What a magnificent and majestic first day's work, and how beautiful it was for the Father, the Word, and the Holy Spirit to all work together in unison to accomplish such a finished product! When God saw what he had made, and the light he had created, he rejoiced and said, "It is good!" (Genesis 1:1–5). There are some, maybe many *"brilliant"* men who do not believe in God (The fool hath said in his heart, There is no God (Psalms 14:1, 53:1); and therefore they do not believe he has created anything—it all just happened. One day, one of them visited Albert Einstein, and he saw a model ship on his desk and asked him if he made it. Albert said "no, no one made it, it just happened." The man said, "but that's impossible!" Albert said "if such a simple object as this model ship could not just happen, how could an entire universe with many perfectly organized and synchronized galaxies and stars, and many living things just happen?" Dr Einstein believed in God, but he believed in the God such as Spinoza believed in, a God who has all power and knowledge, who is infinite and eternal, but does not interfere in the affairs of men.

The second day of creation is somewhat peculiar. Genesis 1:6–8 says:

> And God said, Let there be a firmament in the midst of the waters, and let it divide the waters from the waters. And God made the firmament, and divided the waters which were under the firmament from the waters which were above the

firmament: and it was so. And God called the firmament Heaven. And there was evening and there was morning, a second day.

The information used here to describe the happenings of the second day were taken from the book, *"The Genesis Flood"* by John C. Whitcomb and Henry Morris. That is a book worth reading. The world God made was formed by water (2 Peter 3:5). After God formed the world, it was completely immersed in water. It wasn't until the third day's work that God separated the dry land from the seas (Genesis 1:9–13). Later (about 1,656 years later), the earth was once again immersed in water by the universal flood. It was the second day of creation that helps us to see where all the water came from that caused that flood, along with the fountains of the earth erupting (Genesis 7:10–12).

It was on this day of the creation God separated the waters that covered the earth from the waters that he placed above the earth—that is, above the firmament, or above the heavens. That means there was as much water above the earth, or in the heavens, as there was in the earth's seas and oceans. The water above the earth could not have been contained in clouds; no cloud could contain that much water. Also, at that early time it had never rained on the earth (Genesis 2:5) —so there were no clouds. I have read the works of some very intelligent scientists who are Christians, and they believe the Bible to be what it is— the Word of God. They believe that the water that was above the earth was in the form of a massive water vapor shield that protected the earth from the direct radiation of the sun. That would have created a greenhouse effect resulting in a moderate temperature throughout the earth—day and night. Remember, when Adam and Eve were created they never wore clothes, and they slept without clothes (Genesis 2:25). If the water vapor shield view is correct, and I believe it is, that would explain why there are massive coalbeds in the now ice-covered frozen Antarctic, and why there are innumerable mastodons, tropical animals, and tropical vegetation buried in ice in the remote areas of Siberia.

Those same scientists believe that when the water vapor shield broke it caused the forty-day rain that flooded the world—quite a reasonable conclusion. When it broke it quickly flooded the entire world, and at the same time it immediately caused the earth to depend on direct radiation from the sun. Since there was practically no radiation from the sun whatsoever to warm the areas at the north and south poles of the planet, those areas immediately became frozen wastelands of nothing but ice. That all happened so quickly that the mastodons that were living in present day Siberia were flash-frozen while they were still eating grass and flowers, and they had such in their mouths and in their stomachs when they were discovered many years later. Mastodons were tropical animals, and they depended on enormous amounts of vegetation for their survival. I have read in periodicals that when Siberian natives find a frozen mastodon they cut it up in pieces and feed the meat to their dogs. (Incidentally, scientists have said that there is more ivory in Siberia than there is in both Africa and India combined.) Is there a better explanation as to how the North Pole and the South Pole very quickly became frozen wastelands?

On the third day God separated the waters that were upon the earth, and that created the dry land and the seas. He also created vegetation, and until the flood that was all men and animals ate (Genesis 1:29–30). On that day the Lord prepared the world for all the living creatures that would dwell upon it (Genesis 1:9–3). God gave them something to eat, and plenty of it.

On the fourth day God created the sun, the moon, and the stars (Genesis 1:14–19). Their purpose was to generate heat and light—or become the power source that was necessary for life to exist on earth. They were also created to establish a way to measure the time and the seasons. Time is something we know very little about. When Einstein wrote his theory of relativity, he said that time was relative, and would vary, or be different between things moving and things stationary, and time would be influenced by the force of gravity. He said time would pass more slowly with a very heavy gravitational force, and faster with light or no gravity. He was proven correct. I have read where the clocks in the GPS satellites must be *adjusted* every day, or there would be a six-mile error in the distance they measured for moving objects on earth, all because there is no gravitational force in space. What is time? We just do not know much about it. Moses wrote:

> And God said, Let there be lights in the firmament of heaven to divide the day from the night; and let them be for signs, and for seasons, and for days and years: and let them be for lights in the firmament of heaven to give light upon the earth: and it was so. And God made the two great lights; the greater light to rule the day, and the lesser light to rule the night: he made the stars also. And God set them in the firmament of heaven to give light upon the earth, and to rule over the day and over the night, and to divide the light from the darkness: and God saw that it was good. And there was evening and there was morning, a fourth day. (Genesis 1:14–19)

The Scriptures explain in some detail how and why he created the sun and the moon, both very important to the creation (the sun for light and heat and the moon to control the tides). The creation of the stars is summed up in just five words: "He made the stars also" (Genesis 1:16). The sun is an amazing part of God's creation. It is a controlled nuclear power-plant that is burning itself out at the rate of 4,000 pounds of nuclear fuel every second. The earth receives only a very small part of the energy the sun produces, the rest of that energy dissipates into empty space. The sun must be extremely large to be able to burn so much mass in one second, and for so many thousands of years, with no visible sign of it getting smaller.

After God created the stars, he counted them and called them by their names. The Psalmist wrote, "He counteth the number of the stars; He calleth them all by their names" (Psalms 147:4). The Bible is amazing! Isaiah wrote about the earth being round some seven hundred years before Christ. It is written in Isaiah:

> Have ye not known? have yet not heard? hath it not been told you from the beginning? have ye not understood from the foundations of the earth? It is he that sitteth above the circle of the earth, and the inhabitants thereof are as grasshoppers; that stretcheth out the heavens as a curtain, and spreadeth them out as a tent to dwell in. (Isaiah 40:21–22)

It was Job who noticed the great northern void, and he also knew that God had hung the earth upon nothing, hinting of the gravitational force from the sun that controls the position of the earth (which is as close to nothing—that is nothing observable—as it can get). Job said, "He stretcheth out the north over empty space, and hangeth the earth upon nothing" (Job 26:7).

On the fifth day God created all the fish and all the other things that live in the sea, including the whales and the great sea-monsters. He also created the birds (Genesis 1:20–23) and all things that fly in the heavens. He gave them the commandment to be fruitful and multiply, and they all got that message loud and clear (Genesis 1:21–23).

The sixth day was a very special day, for that was the day God created all the animals—and Adam, or man (Genesis 1:24–31). Man was the only living creature that God created in his own image, and that made them his children. Men are not animals, they did not come from animals, they are God's children, and they have the spirit of God living in them. I have often wondered why God has blesses us, the people living on his planet, with so many beautiful and wonderful things to enjoy. Paul wrote, "Charge them that are rich in this present world, that they be not highminded, nor have their hope set on the uncertainty of riches, but on God, who giveth us richly all things to enjoy" (1 Timothy 6:17). Why does God bless us so much? Because that is how much he loves us. Next question: Why does he love us so much? The answer, because we are his children, and God loves all those to whom he has given life.

God rested on the seventh day, and that day was called the Sabbath (Genesis 2:1–3). That was the day God commanded all men to rest from their works just as God rested from his. To break the Sabbath and work on that Day was a capital crime demanding the death of the transgressor (Exodus 31:14).

The Sabbath day is one event in the Old Testament that is yet to be fulfilled, and yet it is fulfilled every time a saint leaves this world to go home to be with their Father—That is the time when they enter into their eternal rest (Hebrews 4:4–11). However, the Sabbath will be perfectly and completely fulfilled when Jesus comes again and all of God's children are resurrected from their tombs to go to their eternal home, or rest, with their Father in heaven. The law that governed the Sabbath did not go into effect until the Law of Moses was established, and that was the time when God gave Israel the Ten Commandments. The law governing the Sabbath was the fourth of the Ten Commandments. The Gentiles have never been under the Law of Moses, nor have they ever been commanded to keep the Sabbath day (Psalms 147:19–20). The system of a seven-day week is still maintained to this day throughout the entire world.

From the description of the creation we can begin to understand why God condemned Adam for what he had done, and why he must die. The world God created was very precious to him. It was perfect in every way, and it was all given to Adam. When Adam transgressed the law of his Father knowing full well that the penalty for such and action was death, he condemned and destroyed something God treasured. Since the creation had been given to Adam as his own possession, we see why it was condemned with him. But what was God going to do? He had a plan, for he knew before he ever created the world that sin would come into his perfect world and condemn everything he made.

God had the plan for his creation in his mind from the very beginning, and that included the plan to save his new world from any evil force that could threaten it. Therefore, God was fully prepared for what happened when Adam sinned, and he did not go into a panic-mode and start frantically trying to undo the problem Adam caused. The correction for Adam's transgression, and the restoration of all things, had to be accomplished according to the righteousness and holiness of God—all sin must be dealt with and punished according to God's Word, and holiness.

After God declared the condemnation that must fall upon Adam, upon Eve, upon Satan, and upon the entire creation because of Adam's trespass, in very few words he also prophesied the events that would correct the problem Adam's sin had caused. God was going to restore his creation back into its original beauty and perfection, but that new world would not be a physical world: it would be a spiritual world. God's plan would also allow all men back into His fellowship, and it would offer them eternal life in his new world. God would accomplish all of that through the cross—the cross would take away Adam's sin by annulling its consequences, it would offer forgiveness to all men for their own sins (that is, the sins they themselves had committed), and it would create the kingdom of heaven, the place where God's children would live with their Father forever. In other words, the Son of God took away the sins of the world (John 1:29). God did all of that in a righteous and holy way that was carried out according to the holiness and the righteousness of the Almighty. No sin was ever just overlooked or ignored; every sin was punished with the proper and just penalty. Moses wrote:

> And Jehovah God said unto the serpent, Because thou hast done this, cursed art thou above all cattle, and above every beast of the field; upon thy belly shalt thou go, and dust shalt thou eat all the days of thy life: and I will put enmity between thee and the woman, and between thy seed and her seed: he shall bruise thy head, and thou shalt bruise his heel. Unto the woman he said, I will greatly multiply thy pain and thy conception; in pain shalt bring forth children; and thy desire shall be to thy husband, and he shall rule over thee. And unto Adam he said, Because thou hast hearkened unto the voice of thy wife, and hast eaten of the tree, of which I commanded thee, saying, Thou shalt not eat of it: cursed is the ground for thy sake; in toil shalt thou eat of it all the days of thy life; thorns also and thistles shall it bring forth to thee; and thou shalt eat the herb of the field; in the sweat of thy face shalt thou eat bread, till thou return unto the ground; for out of it wast thou taken: for dust thou art, and unto dust shalt thou return. And the man called his wife's name Eve; because she was the mother of all living. (Genesis 3:14–20)

The serpent that deceived Eve was going to receive a lethal blow to the head for what he had done, and it would be struck by the Son of man, who is Jesus. That blow to the serpent's head would kill the serpent. In that process the Son of man himself would be injured (on the cross). However, the injury Jesus suffered during his crucifixion would be completely healed by his resurrection. But the lethal blow to Satan's head killed him and took away his power. Hebrews 2:14–15 says, "Since then the children are sharers in flesh and blood, he also himself in like manner partook of the same; that through death he might bring to nought him that had the power of death, that is, the devil; and might deliver all them who through fear of death were all their lifetime subject to bondage."

The blow to the Son of man's heel was not a fatal blow, it could be healed. It was caused by his death on the cross, and it was healed by his resurrection from the tomb. It was by Jesus' sacrifice on the cross and his resurrection that Satan received his death blow. Throughout Jesus' entire life Satan tried to either tempt him to sin (Matthew 4:1), or to kill him with death. After Satan finally did kill Jesus by tempting evil men to nail him to a cross and let him die, he and his evil angels rejoiced—They had finally conquered their arch enemy! Not even Satan believed that the resurrection from the dead was possible. Satan did not realize that by killing Jesus he had actually executed himself, and all of his evil angels that fell with him (2 Peter 2:4; Jude 6). When Jesus was raised from the tomb Satan lost all of his power, and both spiritual death and physical death were abolished (2 Timothy 1:8–10).

Jesus called the new immortal life he gave to us by his resurrection *"life abundantly"* (John 10:10), and Paul called it *"life indeed"* (1 Timothy 6:19). Life abundantly means more life than is necessary, and life indeed means real, genuine life that cannot get any better. Therefore, Christians should have no fear of death or judgment, because for all believers in Christ both of those terrors have been abolished. Christians die when they are baptized, and that is also when they are judged. When a person is baptized because they truly believe in God and that Jesus is the Christ, God's only begotten Son, at that moment they experience the only death and the only judgment they will ever encounter. The judgment that God declares to the saved is that they have become the holy and righteous sons of God, and God says to them, "Well done, good and faithful servant: thou hast been faithful over a few things, I will set thee over many things; enter thou into the joy of thy lord" (Matthew 25:21).

CHAPTER 4

※

HOW COULD ANOTHER MAN ANNUL THE CONSEQUENCE OF ADAM'S SIN, ABOLISH DEATH, AND RESTORE ALL THINGS TO THEIR FORMER GLORY?

IT WAS ONE MAN'S sin that condemned the entire creation and sentenced every living creature in it to death. It was another Man who annulled the first man's sin by terminating the consequences of his disobedience and abolishing death (2 Timothy 1:10). To understand how a man could have the power to accomplish such a feat we must first understand who that Man was, and then what he did that accomplished such an impossible task. The two men we are speaking of had the same Father, and therefore they were brothers. One of the brothers was called Adam, and he was the first son of God (Luke 3:38). The other Brother's name is Jesus, and he is the only begotten Son of God (John 1:18, 3:16). The first brother yielded to self-indulgence and sinned; his trespass brought sin and death into a perfect world where glory, peace, perfection, love, and righteousness thrived. The other Brother, by His own self-denial died on a cross to take away the trespass his brother had committed, and by his sacrifice he restored the world back to its original beauty, glory, and perfection—offering eternal life to all men—and much more. By Jesus' righteous act of holy obedience, he saved all men from the sin and death Adam brought into the world by his unholy disobedience, and he brought justification of life to all men (Romans 5:18). Paul wrote in his Roman letter, "So then as through one trespass the judgment came unto all men to condemnation; even so through one act of righteousness the free gift came unto all men to justification of life" (Romans 5:18).

It sounds strange that such a terrible and forceful thing such as death could be abolished, but Jesus did exactly that when he eliminated it with his cross and resurrection. That Man, who is the Word, came into the world as the Son of man and the Son of God, and he lived a perfect, flawless, and holy life. Then he offered that life to God from a cross as the perfect sacrifice (sin-offering) that truly took away all the sins of the world (John 1:29). It was Jesus who paid in full for all the damage Adam's trespass had caused, and by his holy and righteous act of obedience he restored the creation to its formal glory by creating a new world, a spiritual world. Even though that world is yet to come (2 Peter 3:13), it is a world that already exists, and it is called the kingdom of God (Mark 1:15), the kingdom of heaven (Matthew 4:17), and the church (Matthew 16:18).

It is amazing that one man's trespass could condemn the entire creation and sentence all men to death. It is just as amazing that another Man's holy righteous act of obedience could immediately abolish that transgression by assuming full responsibility for it—by agreeing to bear the guilt and the shame it had created—and, by paying in full for all the damage it had caused. Then that Man restored everything Adam's sin had corrupted back to its original beauty, glory, and perfection. How could one Man do that? Why would God accept the death of one Man as a sacrifice to forgive the sin of another man, and take away all the sins of many men—and by that same sacrifice offer all men the free gift of eternal life? What could one Man have to offer that was of such great value that it would wipe out a transgression that was so powerful, and so deadly, that it could have destroyed the creation and sentenced the entire human population to death?

There was only one Man who could offer such a sacrifice, his name is Jesus, and he accomplished that wonderful endeavor by sacrificing his own life on a cross to pay the ransom that was required to take away all the sins of the world, including Adam's sin (Matthew 20:28; 1 Timothy 2:6). That Man was Jehovah God himself in a human body (Colossians 2:9), and he was the Word, the Creator of all worlds who became flesh (John 1:1–3, 14) and it is He who became the Son of God and the Son of man!

Jesus had many titles, and they all referred to who he was. In the Old Testament he was called the Messiah (John 1:41, 4:25). In the New Testament he is called the Christ, both names denoting Him to be the Anointed one of God. He was called Immanuel, which means "God with us" (Matthew 1:23) Luke wrote:

> And he came to Nazareth, where he had been brought up: and he entered, as his custom was, into the synagogue on the sabbath day, and stood up to read. And there was delivered unto him the book of the prophet Isaiah. And he opened the book, and found the place where it was written, The Spirit of the Lord is upon me, Because he anointed me to preach good tidings to the poor: He hath sent me to proclaim release to the captives, And recovering of sight to the blind, To set at liberty them that are bruised, To proclaim the acceptable year of the Lord. And he closed the book, and gave it back to the attendant, and sat

down: and the eyes of all in the synagogue were fastened on him. And he began to say unto them, To-day hath this scripture been fulfilled in your ears. (Luke 4:16–21)

And Peter opened his mouth and said, Of a truth I perceive that God is no respecter of persons: but in every nation he that feareth him, and worketh righteousness, is acceptable to him. The word which he sent unto the children of Israel, preaching good tidings of peace by Jesus Christ (He is Lord of all.)—that saying ye yourselves know, which was published throughout all Judaea, beginning from Galilee, after the baptism which John preached; even Jesus of Nazareth, how God anointed him with the Holy Spirit and with power: who went about doing good, and healing all that were oppressed of the devil; for God was with him. (Acts 10:34–38)

In the Old Testament it was the prophets, the priests, and the kings who were the anointed men of God. But in the New Testament it is Jesus who is the anointed King of kings and Lord of lords (Revelation 17:14); the Prophet of the Most High God (Matthew 21:5–11); and the High Priest of God (Hebrews 4:14–16). There was only one other person in the Bible who was equal to Jesus as the anointed King and High Priest of God, his name was Melchizedek. The descriptions of those two men, Melchizedek and the Christ are so similar that they must be one and the same Man. Let us view who they were:

In the Old Testament Melchizedek was the king of peace, the king of righteousness, and the priest of the Most High God. He was *made like unto the Son of God* (Hebrews 7:3), and that was before there was a Son of God, other than Adam—and

Adam was not a priest or a king. In the New Testament Jesus truly was the Son of God (Matthew 27:54; Mark 1:1). Jesus is the Prince of Peace (Isaiah 9:6), the King of Righteousness (1 Corinthians 1:30; Jeremiah 23:5–6), the King of kings and the Lord of lords (Revelation 17:14), and the Priest of the Most High God (Hebrews 6:20). Those are the descriptions of the One who came into this world as the Son of man and the Son of God to become our Priest, and our Savior. He came to redeem God's world and the human family from the consequences of Adam's transgression by annulling it, and by restoring the creation back into its original beauty and perfection. He also came to deliver all men from the punishment that was due to fall upon them for their own sins (that is, the sins they themselves had committed). In other words, Jesus came to take away all the sins of the world (John 1:29).

In Genesis 14:1–24, four very powerful kings had attacked the five kings of Sodom, Gomorrah, and three other villages. Abraham's nephew, Lot, lived in Sodom. Those kings had been paying taxes for twelve years to the powerful kings who had attacked them. The thirteenth year they rebelled and quit paying, for they could pay no more (Genesis 14:4–5). Abraham's nephew, Lot, and all his family, who lived in Sodom, were taken captive with the rest of the city. All their possessions were stolen. The possessions of the other four cities were taken as well. When Abraham was told about that (Genesis 14:13–14), Abraham took his 318 trained men and attacked the oppressors, the four kings, by night. He defeated them and redeemed Lot and all the stolen goods. The two kings of Sodom and Gomorrah wanted to reward Abraham, but Abraham refused their offer. He did not want anyone thinking it was they who had made him rich. God was well pleased with what Abraham had done, and a very unusual person—perhaps the most unusual person who is mentioned in the Bible—appeared to Abraham and blessed him. His name was Melchizedek. That person only appears here, when he blessed

Abraham, and Abraham paid tithes to him. It is possible that Melchizedek appeared at other times (such as in Genesis 18), but if so he was never called by the name Melchizedek.

Melchizedek was both priest and king. Moses described that rare meeting between Melchizedek and Abraham in the book of Genesis, where he wrote:

> And Melchizedek king of Salem brought forth bread and wine: and he was priest of God Most High. And he blessed him, and said, Blessed be Abram of God Most High, possessor of heaven and earth: and blessed be God Most High, who hath delivered thine enemies into thy hand. And he gave him a tenth of all. (Genesis 14:18–20)

There is only one other place in the Old Testament that mentions Melchizedek (Psalms 110:4), and that verse says that the priesthood of Jesus shall be after the order of the priesthood of Melchizedek. If Jesus' priesthood is after the order of Melchizedek's priesthood, then their priesthoods were identical. Aaron, a Levite and Moses' brother was the first priest that Israel had. But Aaron's priesthood could not represent the priesthood of Jesus because their priesthoods were not identical. Both Aaron, as the priest of Israel, and his priesthood had many flaws, (which will be discussed shortly). However, both Melchizedek's priesthood and Jesus' priesthood had no flaws. Their priesthoods were perfect, holy, and righteous in every respect. Jesus as Priest, after the order of Melchizedek's priesthood, means that just as Jesus was perfect, holy, and righteous—so also was Melchizedek perfect, holy, and righteous—In fact he was the King of Righteousness (Hebrews 7:1–2). Please consider that statement seriously.

When Abraham met Melchizedek after his great victory, it was Abraham who was blessed by Melchizedek, and it was

Melchizedek to whom Abraham paid tithes (Hebrews 7:1-2). Both of those acts declared that it was Melchizedek who was the greater man. But when Abraham lived on the earth, the father of the faithful, and the one to whom all the blessings of God had been promised, wasn't he the greatest living man? Even heaven is called "*Abraham's bosom*" (Luke 16:22). When Abraham met Melchizedek, Abraham was the father of the faithful (Galatians 3:7–9), and he was one of the greatest of all men who had ever lived on the earth.

Jesus said that among all men who were born of a woman there had not arisen a man greater than John the Baptist (Matthew 11:11). But Abraham was just as great, just not greater. (I wonder where Jesus placed himself when he made that statement, for Jesus was born of a woman. Jesus' must have meant that there had never arisen a man greater than John the Baptist, but there had arisen many men who were just as great). But Melchizedek was greater because he was the Lord himself in human form. Melchizedek was not born of a woman; he had no father, he had no mother, and he had no genealogy. He had no beginning of days or end of life, which means he was eternal. He was the Word, the Creator of all worlds, in human form.

Many questions have been raised about his identity. Who was that man? How could he be the priest of the Most High God and king when no place on earth can be established as to where he was a priest, or over what city he ruled as king? Melchizedek was the king of Salem, and Salem is not a place—Salem is peace (and righteousness) (Hebrews 7:1-2). But it was not peace among men; it was peace with God. What people, or nation, did Melchizedek represent as a priest and king? Who appeared before God through Melchizedek? If he was a priest of the God Most High, then all men, without exception, including Aaron, had only one access to God: it was through Melchizedek. If that was not so then it causes a problem with Melchizedek being a priest who determined the order of Christ as Priest, and Melchizedek's priesthood determining the order of Jesus' priesthood. Jesus said no man shall come to the Father but through him (John 14:6). Therefore, during the time of Melchizedek no man could appear before the Father except through Melchizedek.

For Melchizedek to be both priest and king he must have had a kingdom and a priesthood—but where were they and what were they? Some have said he was king and priest in Jerusalem, but Scripture does not say Jerusalem, it says Salem, and Salem means "peace." It also means "righteousness" (Hebrews 7:1-2). It is possible Jerusalem did not exist at that time (only about five-hundred years after the flood), and if it did exist it would be an insignificant little village. But Salem means peace, and righteousness, and there was no place on earth called by either of those names.

Melchizedek is mentioned seven times in the book of Hebrews, and it is that letter that identifies who he was:

> For this Melchizedek, king of Salem, priest of God Most High, who met Abraham returning from the slaughter of the kings and blessed him, to whom also Abraham divided a tenth part of all (being first, by interpretation, King of righteousness, and then also King of Salem, which is King of peace; without father, without mother, without genealogy, having neither beginning of days nor end of life, but made like unto the Son of God), abideth a priest continually. Now consider how great this man was, unto whom Abraham, the patriarch, gave a tenth out of the chief spoils. And they indeed of the sons of Levi that receive the priest's office have commandment to take tithes of the people according to the law, that is, of their brethren, though these have come out of the loins of Abraham: but he whose genealogy is not

counted from them hath taken tithes of Abraham, and hath blessed him that hath the promises. But without any dispute the less is blessed of the better. And here men that die receive tithes; but there one, of whom it is witnessed that he liveth. (Hebrews 7:1–8)

That man, Melchizedek, can be none other than the Word or the Lord himself in human form, because everything that was said about Melchizedek can also be said about Jesus. Melchizedek and Jesus were both kings and priests, and no other person in the entire Bible has ever filled both of those offices except Jesus and Melchizedek. Melchizedek was the king of righteousness and the king of peace. Jesus is the King of kings and Lord of lords (Revelation 17:14), the King of righteousness, and the King (or Prince) of peace just as Jeremiah and Isaiah have described him. Jeremiah wrote:

Behold, the days come, saith Jehovah, that I will raise unto David a righteous Branch, and he shall reign as king and deal wisely, and shall execute justice and righteousness in the land. In his days Judah shall be saved, and Israel shall dwell safely; and this is his name whereby he shall be called: Jehovah our righteousness. (Jeremiah 23:5–6)

Jeremiah said that Jesus, the branch of David, shall reign as "King," and that his name shall be called "Jehovah our righteousness." Therefore, Jesus is Jehovah, he is the King of righteousness, and he has all power and authority to execute justice and righteousness. But so did Melchizedek. Paul wrote that Jesus was made to be the Christians' righteousness (1 Corinthians 1:30).

For a person to be the king of righteousness he must not only be holy and righteous himself, but he must also be the standard-bearer who rules over righteousness. He is the one who determines who is righteous and who is not, and what is righteous and what is not. There is no man who has ever had such authority but Jesus and Melchizedek (Hebrews 7:1–3).

Melchizedek was also the king of peace, which means he ruled over peace, and he was the standard of peace—But the peace that Melchizedek ruled over, and the peace that Jesus rules over is not peace among men, or peace among nations—*it is the peace between men and God.* Matthew wrote:

> Think not that I came to send peace on the earth:
> I came not to send peace, but a sword. For I came
> to set a man at variance against his father, and the
> daughter against her mother, and the daughter in
> law against her mother in law: and a man's foes
> shall be they of his own household. (Matthew
> 10:3)

John wrote about the peace we have with God because of Jesus and his coming, when he said, "Peace I leave with you; my peace I give unto you: not as the world giveth, give I unto you. Let not your heart be troubled, neither let it be fearful" (John 14:27). Paul wrote, "Being therefore justified by faith, we have peace with God through our Lord Jesus Christ; through whom also we have had our access by faith into this grace wherein we stand; and we rejoice in hope of the glory of God" (Romans 5:1–2). Jesus is the King of peace or the Prince of peace, as Isaiah has written:

> For unto us a child is born, unto us a son is given;
> and the government shall be upon his shoulder:
> and his name shall be called Wonderful, Coun-
> sellor, Mighty God, Everlasting Father, Prince of
> Peace." (Isaiah 9:6)

When Paul wrote his letter to the Ephesians, he told his Ephesian brethren that Jesus is our peace:

> But now in Christ Jesus ye that once were far off are made nigh in the blood of Christ. For he is our peace, who made both one, and brake down the middle wall of partition, having abolished in his flesh the enmity, even the law of commandments contained in ordinances; that he might create in himself of the two one new man, so making peace; and might reconcile them both in one body unto God through the cross, having slain the enmity thereby: and he came and preached peace to you that were far off, and peace to them that were nigh: for through him we both have our access in one Spirit unto the Father. So then ye are no more strangers and sojourners, but ye are fellow-citizens with the saints, and of the household of God, being built upon the foundation of the apostles and prophets, Christ Jesus himself being the chief corner stone; in whom each several building, fitly framed together, groweth into a holy temple in the Lord; in whom ye also are builded together for a habitation of God in the Spirit. (Ephesians 2:13–22)

Just as Melchizedek was the priest of God Most High, so also is Jesus. Jesus was chosen by God to fill that office after the order of Melchizedek (Psalms 110:4). Hebrews 5:5–6 says, "So Christ also glorified not himself to be made a high priest, but he that spake unto him, Thou art my Son, this day have I begotten thee: as he saith also in another place, Thou art a priest for ever After the order of Melchizedek." The point the writer of Hebrews was making is—that just as God had declared Jesus to be his Son, he has also affirmed that he has appointed him to be High Priest forever after the order of Melchizedek.

There are other words that describe Melchizedek that also describe Jesus. Just as Melchizedek was without father, without mother, without genealogy, having neither beginning of days or end of life, so also was Jesus. As the Word, Jesus was in the beginning with God (John 1:1–2), and He was the great *"I AM"* before Abraham was born (John 8:58). So, it must have been Jesus, the Word, who appeared to Abraham in a human body as Melchizedek.

There are many questions about Melchizedek we cannot answer unless we view him as the Word of God in human form— For instance, what and where were his kingdom and his priesthood? What people did he serve as priest of God Most High? How did they approach God through him? Was there any person on this earth who could approach God without approaching him through Melchizedek, priest of the Most High God? If so, what was the purpose of his priesthood, and how could he determine the order of the priesthood of Christ (John 14:6)? Where did he come from to meet Abraham? How did he know about Abraham's great victory over the five kings, and why did it matter to him? Where did Melchizedek go after he left Abraham? What did he do with one-tenth of the spoils of war Abraham gave him? (Hebrews 7:1-2). Melchizedek was not some obscure unimportant person who was sent by God to bless Abraham and be the type of the Christ's priesthood, and then just vanish from history until the book of Hebrews was written. Maybe this is the answer to the question, "Who was Melchizedek and where did he come from? Where did he rule as priest and king?"

In the beginning God created a perfect world where sin did not exist (Genesis 1:31). In such a world all of God's children and the entire creation had a perfect relationship with God. There was no need for a go-between, a bridge, or a priest between man and God because God and his entire world had perfect harmony and fellowship with each other without one. But when Adam sinned, he died, and he was cut off from God. By his sin the entire human family stood condemned (Romans 8:20–22). Adam's sin caused God to withdraw his presence from the holy world he had created (Genesis 1:31) because Adam's sin made it quite unholy. It had been totally contaminated by sin. Adam broke God's heart in the process and he pierced him through with many sorrows (Genesis 6:6). From that time on if a man wanted to approach the Almighty, he had to be invited by God to do so—but! —there would have to be someone between God and man to represent both parties in any such communications between them, for because of sin no man could have direct access to God. Any man who wanted to approach God had to have someone to represent him to the Almighty (John 14:6). That person also had to be just as holy and righteous as God himself is holy and righteous, or even he could not approach the Almighty, not even for himself. He would have to be like God, as well as being a man—a man like all other men (Hebrews 5:1–2). A priest is a bridge between two points, and in this case those two points are man and God. Does that say something about Melchizedek?

After Moses became God's man and his law had been established, Aaron, Moses' brother, was appointed by God to be the high priest of Israel. But Aaron represented only the nation of Israel, and not the Gentiles (Psalms 147:19–20). During the period of time between Adam and Moses, who was it that represented the people to God? Who represented the Gentiles to God from the time of Moses to Christ? During those periods of time there were many people who wanted fellowship with God—good men such as Enoch, the seventh from Adam (Genesis 5:21–24; Hebrews 11:5; Jude 1:14), Abraham, Noah, Job, and others—including Cornelius in the New Testament (Acts, chapters 10 and 11). Those men shall not be rejected by God just because they had not been born into the nation of Israel. Melchizedek is the only one who could have been their representative. Otherwise, what would be the purpose of even mentioning him? The purpose of Melchizedek being the high priest of the Most High God was to allow men, *all men*, to approach the Almighty through him. Therefore, before Jesus became God's High Priest, was there anyone who could approach God, the Almighty, except through Melchizedek? If no one could appear before God except through Christ, even before he was appointed High Priest (John 14:6), then Melchizedek, who determined the order of the priesthood of Christ, had to have been exactly that same kind of Priest with the same type of priesthood, and no man could appear before God except through him. Melchizedek was the Word in human form.

Jesus is the Word who became flesh (John 1:1–2, 14). After his death on the cross and his resurrection, he was appointed by God to be the King of Israel and the Priest of God Most High. Jesus had to be a man to be appointed to that grand position (Hebrews 5:1–2). But so did Melchizedek. But from the beginning God knew that the Word would become flesh—a man. Therefore, even before Jesus died on the cross God considered him to be qualified to fill the office of High Priest. So, just as God could forgive sin before Jesus had died on the cross to become our sin offering (2 Samuel 12:13), he could also establish a priesthood between men and God through him. In the mind of God, the cross, and all the blessings that resulted because it, were established facts before he laid the foundation of the world (Ephesians 1:3–4, 1 Peter 1:17–20). Therefore, all the blessings of God that came by the way of the cross could be granted to all men from the time of Adam until the end of time. If this view is correct, and I certainly believe it is, then Melchizedek's kingdom was the eternal kingdom of God—the kingdom of peace, the kingdom of righteousness, and it was the Word (Melchizedek) who was the King and the Priest—the very position to which God appointed Jesus as the reward for his work of redemption after he had been raised from the dead (Matthew 28:16–20).

Melchizedek's kingdom and priesthood were between God and all men who lived between the time of Adam and the resurrection of Jesus. After that, God appointed Jesus as King and High Priest after the order of Melchizedek—and not after the order of Aaron (Hebrews 7:11). Aaron's priesthood was flawed, and the perfect priesthood of Christ could not be reckoned after a priesthood that had many problems, for Christ's priesthood has no problems. It is perfect:

> Now if there was perfection through the Levitical priesthood (for under it hath the people received the law), what further need was there that another priest should arise after the order of Melchizedek, and not be reckoned after the order of Aaron? For the priesthood being changed, there is made of necessity a change also of the law. For he of whom these things are said belongeth to another tribe, from which no man hath given attendance at the altar. For it is evident that our Lord hath sprung out of Judah; as to which tribe Moses spake nothing concerning priests. And what we say is yet more abundantly evident, if after the likeness of Melchizedek there ariseth another priest, who hath been made, not after the law of a carnal commandment, but after the power of an endless life: for it is witnessed of him, Thou art a priest for ever After the order of Melchizedek. For there is a disannulling of a foregoing commandment because of its weakness and unprofitableness (for the law made nothing perfect), and a bringing in thereupon of a better hope, through which we draw nigh unto God. And inasmuch as it is not without the taking of an oath for they indeed have been made priests without an oath;

but he with an oath by him that saith of him, The Lord sware and will not repent himself, Thou art a priest for ever); by so much also hath Jesus become the surety of a better covenant. And they indeed have been made priests many in number, because that by death they are hindered from continuing: but he, because he abideth for ever, hath his priesthood unchangeable. Wherefore also he is able to save to the uttermost them that draw near unto God through him, seeing he ever liveth to make intercession for them. For such a high priest became us, holy, guileless, undefiled, separated from sinners, and made higher than the heavens; who needeth not daily, like those high priests, to offer up sacrifices, first for his own sins, and then for the sins of the people: for this he did once for all, when he offered up himself. For the law appointeth men high priests, having infirmity; but the word of the oath, which was after the law, appointeth a Son, perfected forever more. (Hebrews 7:11–28)

If Jesus' priesthood could not be reckoned after the order of the priesthood of Aaron because Aaron's priesthood was flawed, how could his priesthood be reckoned after the order of the priesthood of Melchizedek if his priesthood was also flawed? That means that Melchizedek, his kingdom, and his priesthood had to be absolutely perfect, holy, righteous, and sinless, without beginning and without end, and it was only the Word who satisfied those traits.

Jesus could not be a priest after the order of Aaron because Aaron died, and someone had to take his place. When the one who replaced him died it was necessary to replace him, and so that became a reoccurring event. Jesus was the one and only person who ever filled his office as Priest (from Adam to this present time). There were none before him and there shall not be any after him as Priest of the Most High God. Also, because Aaron was a sinner and Jesus was not, Aaron could not typify Jesus as priest, nor could his priesthood typify the priesthood of Christ (Hebrews 7:17–28). Doesn't that mean that Melchizedek had to be a holy, righteous, and sinless man—a man who had no beginning and who would have no end—to represent Jesus in his priesthood? Such a man, other than the Word, has never existed.

This might present a question. When Aaron was the high priest for Israel and he could approach God only one day a year on the Day of Atonement by entering the Most Holy Place with the blood of an animal, first for his own sins, and then for the sins of the people (Hebrews 9:6–7), who was it that Aaron appeared before in the Most Holy Place? Or, who did he appear before so he would be permitted to enter the Most Holy Place? —especially when he presented his own sacrifice to God first, for his own sins? Not even Aaron, as a sinner, could present his own sacrifice directly to God without going through a priest, and that priest was Melchizedek. If all of this is true, it seems in this area that things did not change much for Jesus after his resurrection. Before, and after Jesus' resurrection, he was King of Righteousness, King of Peace, Priest of the Most High God, and there was no one who appeared before God the Almighty except through him.

Jesus said, "I am the way, and the truth, and the life: no one cometh unto the Father, but by me" (John 14:6). When Jesus spoke those words he had not yet gone to the cross, he had not been raised from the dead to establish his priesthood, and he had not been appointed High Priest. So, has there ever been a time, except in the days before sin came into the world when anyone could appear before the Almighty without going through a priest, or through Christ, the Word? Jesus is the only access to God that there has ever been from Adam, to Moses, to this present time.

He said so in John 14:6. The book of Hebrews might shed a little light on this question:

> Now these things having been thus prepared, the priests go in continually into the first tabernacle, accomplishing the services; but into the second the high priest alone, once in the year, not without blood, which he offereth for himself, and for the errors of the people: the Holy Spirit this signifying, that the way into the holy place hath not yet been made manifest, while the first tabernacle is yet standing; which is a figure for the time present; according to which are offered both gifts and sacrifices that cannot, as touching the conscience, make the worshipper perfect. (Hebrews 9:6–9)

Before Christ and his resurrection the way into the Holy Place was closed. Even when it was open on that one day a year, the Day of Atonement, the blood of an animal, or the sacrifices that were presented in it, did not offer perfection. Hebrews 10:1–4 says:

> For the law having a shadow of the good things to come, not the very image of the things, can never with the same sacrifices year by year, which they offer continually, make perfect them that draw nigh. Else would they not have ceased to be offered? because the worshippers, having been once cleansed, would have had no more consciousness of sins. But in those sacrifices there is a remembrance made of sins year by year. For it is impossible that the blood of bulls and goats should take away sins.

But the sacrifice of Jesus on the cross and his priesthood do offer perfection. Hebrews 9:11–12 says:

> But Christ having come a high priest of the good things to come, through the greater and more perfect tabernacle, not made with hands, that is to say, not of this creation, nor yet through the blood of goats and calves, but through his own blood, entered in once for all into the holy place, having obtained eternal redemption. For if the blood of goats and bulls, and the ashes of a heifer sprinkling them that have been defiled, sanctify unto the cleanness of the flesh: how much more shall the blood of Christ, who through the eternal Spirit offered himself without blemish unto God, cleanse your conscience from dead works to serve the living God?

The way into the true Holy Place where God actually lives was not made manifest until the day Jesus died on the cross. That was the day when the sin problem was perfectly solved, paid for, and corrected. The sins of the world had been taken away (John 1:29), and the veil between the holy place, and the Most Holy Place, was ripped in two from top to bottom—declaring it was God who had ripped it open. On that day the way into the Holy Place of God, the real Most Holy of Holies where God lives, was opened to all men for all time, but only through Jesus; and it all depended on Jesus' resurrection. Therefore, any person who comes to Jesus in faith believing that he is the Son of God, that he had died on the cross for them, and he was resurrected (Romans 10:9) would be saved. Matthew said:

> And Jesus cried again with a loud voice, and yielded up his spirit. And behold, the veil of

the temple was rent in two from the top to the bottom; and the earth did quake; and the rocks were rent; and the tombs were opened; and many bodies of the saints that had fallen asleep were raised; and coming forth out of the tombs after his resurrection they entered into the holy city and appeared unto many. Now the centurion, and they that were with him watching Jesus, when they saw the earthquake, and the things that were done, feared exceedingly, saying, Truly this was the Son of God. (Matthew 27:50–54)

Many saints came out of their graves when Jesus died, and after his resurrection they entered Jerusalem to be seen by many of their friends and brethren—the very men who knew they had died. That must have been an event that was seen by many people, especially the Roman soldiers. They had witnessed the earth shaking, the darkness that fell over all the land, and then—the saints coming out of their tombs, and it caused them to tremble, tremble, tremble; and to confess that they had made a terrible mistake—they had crucified the Son of God! (Matthew 27:54).

It was a horrible shame that after they took Jesus down from the cross and things had somewhat returned to normal, some priest went right back into that tabernacle and stitched that veil right back together, once again separating themselves from God—because they failed to see what God had done with the cross of his Son.

There are some who have a problem with God appearing as a man, in a human body, before Jesus was born to Mary as the Son of man. However, God can do whatever he feels is necessary for him to establish and secure his kingdom, and there were occasions when that did happen. One is recorded in Genesis chapter 18. That chapter of Scripture describes a time when the Lord, Jehovah, appeared to Abraham as a man. Genesis 18:1–2 says:

And Jehovah appeared unto him by the oaks of Mamre, as he sat in the tent door in the heat of the day; and he lifted up his eyes and looked, and, lo, three men stood over against him: and when he saw them, he ran to meet them from the tent door, and bowed himself to the earth.

Abraham's greeting was unusual unless Abraham had recognized one of those men as someone he had met before. Abraham had met two kings: Pharaoh, king of Egypt (Genesis 12:10–20), and Abimelech, king of Gerar (Genesis 20:1–5), but there is nothing mentioned about Abraham bowing before either of those kings. Therefore, one of the men Abraham saw before the oaks of Mamre could have been Melchizedek, or the Word in human form, for Abraham would probably not have bowed in such a fashion before just another man. After Abraham had returned from the slaughter of the four kings and he met the kings of Sodom and Gomorrah, and Melchizedek (Genesis 14:16–24), nothing is even mentioned about him bowing before any of them. Maybe, at that time Abraham did not know who Melchizedek truly was.

One of the three men Abraham saw by the oaks of Mamre was Jehovah. The other two were mighty angels—possibly Michael and Gabriel—because one of them started talking to Abraham about what he was about to do, and he addressed himself as *Jehovah*. First, he told Abraham that Sarah was going to have a child, and Sarah laughed. (So did Abraham. See Genesis 17:17). Then, Genesis 18:13–14 says:

And Jehovah said unto Abraham, Wherefore did Sarah laugh, saying, Shall I of a surety bear a child, who am old? Is anything too hard for Jehovah? At the set time I will return unto thee, when the season cometh round, and Sarah shall have a son.

Then, again, it was Jehovah who started discussing with Abraham about what he was going to do to Sodom and Gomorrah. Genesis 18:16–18 says:

> And the men rose up from thence, and looked toward Sodom: and Abraham went with them to bring them on the way. And Jehovah said, Shall I hide from Abraham that which I do; seeing that Abraham shall surely become a great and mighty nation, and all the nations of the earth shall be blessed in him?

But when the three men started toward Sodom and Gomorrah only two of them left, and one of the men, Jehovah, stayed with Abraham and continued the discussion with him. Genesis 19:1 says, "And the two angels came to Sodom at even; and Lot sat in the gate of Sodom: and Lot saw them, and rose up to meet them; and he bowed himself with his face to the earth." Only two of the men (or two angels) left Abraham and went to Sodom, and the third man was not an angel—he was Jehovah! and he continued his discussion with Abraham. As far as we know God did not appear to men as another man very often—but he did here, to Abraham, and he also appeared in human form to Abraham as Melchizedek. It would be interesting to know if Jehovah ever appears as a man in this present world and in this present time to anyone, or for any cause or any reason. If so, it would be impossible for anyone to know such an event had occurred (Matthew 25:34–46). However, we do know the angels are here continually in constant service to God and his saints as they persistently minister to God's people (Hebrews 1:13–14). Therefore, we should be very careful about how we treat other people because some have entertained angels unaware. Hebrews 13:1–2 says, "Let love of the brethren continue. Forget not to show love unto strangers: for thereby some have entertained angels unawares."

Not only is it possible to entertain angels unaware, but it also most certainly happens—The Bible says it happens as they minister to us.

JESUS CAME INTO THE WORLD by being born of a virgin, and with God being his only Father. Isaiah prophesied of his coming when he wrote, "Therefore the Lord himself will give you a sign: behold, a virgin shall conceive, and bear a son, and shall call his name Immanuel" (Isaiah 7:14). Matthew wrote about the fulfillment of that prophecy, "Behold, the virgin shall be with child, and shall bring forth a son, and they shall call his name Immanuel; which is, being interpreted, God with us" (Matthew 1:23). Luke also wrote of the fulfillment of that event:

> Now in the sixth month the angel Gabriel was sent from God unto a city of Galilee, named Nazareth, to a virgin betrothed to a man whose name was Joseph, of the house of David; and the virgin's name was Mary. And he came in unto her, and said, Hail, thou that art highly favored, the Lord is with thee. But she was greatly troubled at the saying, and cast in her mind what manner of salutation this might be. And the angel said unto her, Fear not, Mary: for thou hast found favor with God. And behold, thou shalt conceive in thy womb, and bring forth a son, and shalt call his name JESUS. He shall be great, and shall be called the Son of the Most High: and the Lord God shall give unto him the throne of his father David: and he shall reign over the house of Jacob for ever; and of his kingdom there shall be no end. And Mary said unto the angel, How shall this be, seeing I know not a man? And the angel answered and said unto her, The Holy Spirit shall come upon thee, and the power of the Most High shall

overshadow thee: wherefore also the holy thing which is begotten shall be called the Son of God. (Luke 1:26–35)

The virgin birth of Jesus caused Joseph and Mary many problems. Mary was a virgin, and neither Mary nor Joseph could understand how she could have a child having never known a man. It was Matthew who wrote of the problems that the virgin birth caused them:

Now the birth of Jesus Christ was on this wise: When his mother Mary had been betrothed to Joseph, before they came together she was found with child of the Holy Spirit. And Joseph her husband, being a righteous man, and not willing to make her a public example, was minded to put her away privily. But when he thought on these things, behold, an angel of the Lord appeared unto him in a dream, saying, Joseph, thou son of David, fear not to take unto thee Mary thy wife: for that which is conceived in her is of the Holy Spirit. And she shall bring forth a son; and thou shalt call his name JESUS; for it is he that shall save his people from their sins. Now all this is come to pass, that it might be fulfilled which was spoken by the Lord through the prophet, saying, Behold, the virgin shall be with child, and shall bring forth a son, And they shall call his name Immanuel; which is, being interpreted, God with us. And Joseph arose from his sleep, and did as the angel of the Lord commanded him, and took unto him his wife; and knew her not till she had brought forth a son: and he called his name JESUS. (Matthew 1:18–25)

Joseph and Mary were a young couple who were about to become husband and wife. They had been chosen by God to become the parents of his Son. They were both righteous and godly people, and they were very poor. When Joseph found out that he was about to marry a pregnant woman, and he knew the child she was bearing was not his, he did not know what to do. He could have had her stoned for adultery (Deuteronomy 22:23–24). However, he loved Mary with great passion, and her being pregnant greatly distressed him. Mary told Joseph the truth, that she had not been with a man, and her child had been fathered by the Holy Spirit. Mary told Joseph that she was carrying God's Child, and that she was going to give birth to the Son of God, the Messiah. For some reason Joseph did not believe her. Joseph did not want to hurt Mary beyond the problems they had already experienced. He decided to divorce her quietly, and he was not going to give a reason for putting her away. By the Law of Moses he could do that (Deuteronomy 24:1). The Holy Spirit had to appear to Joseph to convince him that Mary was telling the truth and the child she was carrying truly was the Son of God.

What thoughts must have gone through Mary's and Joseph's minds the moment they fully understood that they had been chosen by God to be the parents of his Son, and that Mary was the woman, the virgin (Isaiah 7:14), who would give birth to the Messiah, the Son of God and the Savior of the world. It was Mary's child who was the very One the whole world had been waiting for, for hundreds of years—and perhaps Joseph and Mary were also waiting for that time to come. What must Joseph have thought about being the father of the Messiah, being responsible for raising him, feeding him, taking care of him, and giving him his education? How could Joseph, a poorly educated carpenter himself (Matthew 13:55–56) teach the Son of God and the Creator of the world anything about life, about facing the problems he knew he would have, or even about death? How did Joseph feel about teaching his Son how to become a carpenter, how to hold a hammer, and how to use a saw when Jesus was the creator of the universe? Jesus was born to Joseph and Mary just as the prophets predicted he would be, and he became exactly what they said he would become: the Son of God, the Christ, and the Savior of the world.

Just as Jesus had tried throughout his ministry to teach his disciples that he came into the world with the definite purpose of going into Jerusalem to be chastised and abused by the religious leaders of Israel, to be beaten, spit upon, nailed to a cross to be left to die (Matthew 16:21–23; Mark 8:31–33; Luke 9:22, 17:25),—and that it could never be any other way (Matthew 26:51–54; John 12:27)—so also he must have continually spoken to Joseph and Mary about those things. I do not think Joseph and Mary wanted to hear what Jesus had to say about the dreadful way his life would end any more than did his apostles. However, they had no choice. I can't imagine how many times Joseph must have told his Son that he had heard enough, and not to speak of those things anymore.

Joseph died somewhere between the year Jesus was twelve and the time he began his ministry, because the last mention of Joseph is in Luke 2:40–52 when Jesus had stayed behind in the temple and amazed the doctors of the Law with his questions and answers. When Jesus was twelve, he knew at that young age who he was. He knew he was the Son of God, and he knew who his real Father was. He knew what his Father's business was: Salvation! He knew what his purpose in life would be. However, Joseph never saw Jesus accomplish his mission. When Jesus went to the cross Joseph was not there, for he had died. I believe God took Joseph home to heaven before Jesus had to go to the cross. God knew the gentle nature of Joseph, and he knew that the cross was a burden Joseph just could not endure to witness— that is, seeing his Son spit on, terribly abused, beaten, scourged, and then nailed to a cross to be lifted up and left to die. Joseph going home to be with God was an act of great mercy on God's part to spare him from seeing his Son being crucified (Isaiah 57:1–2).

However, Mary, Jesus' mother was there when Jesus was crucified (John 19:25). She seems to have stood up strongly against the terrible things she had to witness: her beloved Son being so terribly abused and nailed to a cross and left there to die. Jesus must have prepared Mary well for his crucifixion by continually telling her of all the things that must come to pass, and why. Mary treasured in her heart everything she heard concerning her Son, such as the things she had heard from the shepherds the day Jesus was born (Luke 2:18-19).

It is interesting to note that on the third day after Jesus' crucifixion several women went to the tomb of Jesus to anoint his body. Mary, the mother of Jesus, was not one of those women:

> And when the sabbath was past, Mary Magdalene, and Mary the mother of James, and Salome, bought spices, that they might come and anoint him. And very early on the first day of the week, they come to the tomb when the sun was risen. And they were saying among themselves, Who shall roll us away the stone from the door of the tomb? and looking up, they see that the stone is rolled back: for it was exceeding great. And entering into the tomb, they saw a young man sitting on the right side, arrayed in a white robe; and they were amazed. And he saith unto them, Be not amazed: ye seek Jesus, the Nazarene, who hath been crucified: he is risen; he is not here: behold, the place where they laid him! But go, tell his disciples and Peter, He goeth before you into Galilee: there shall ye see him, as he said unto you. And they went out, and fled from the tomb; for trembling and astonishment had come upon

them: and they said nothing to any one; for they were afraid. (Mark 16:1–8)

Jesus not only taught Mary about the things she should expect to happen when his life came to an end, to prepare her for the terrible event she must witness; he also taught her that on the third day after his crucifixion he would be raised from the dead, and on that day the tomb would be very empty. That is exactly what happened. When the women arrived at the tomb the stone had been rolled away from the mouth of the grave—not to let Jesus out of the tomb, but so the women could look in it to see that Jesus was not there. He was gone! Jesus had risen from the dead on the third day just as he told Mary and all his disciples he would be (Matthew 16:21; Mark 8:31; Luke 9:22). Mary believed Jesus, and that is why she never went to the tomb with the other women to anoint his body—she knew there would not be any body there to anoint.

The other disciples, and even the apostles did not believe that Jesus would be raised from the dead; they were very reluctant to believe such a thing was even possible. Matthew wrote:

> Now when he was risen early on the first day of the week, he appeared first to Mary Magdalene, from whom he had cast out seven demons. She went and told them that had been with him, as they mourned and wept. And they, when they heard that he was alive, and had been seen of her, disbelieved. And after these things he was manifested in another form unto two of them, as they walked, on their way into the country. And they went away and told it unto the rest: neither believed they them. And afterward he was manifested unto the eleven themselves as they sat at meat; and he upbraided them with their unbelief

and hardness of heart, because they believed not them that had seen him after he was risen. (Mark 16:9–14)

Even though the eleven apostles had been with Jesus for over three years (Judas had gone away from them and had hanged himself because of his disbelief) (Matthew 27:3–5), they were still reluctant to believe the Man they were with was really Jesus, their Lord and their Master, and that he had been resurrected. The very day Jesus' disciples were with him on the mount, just moments before he ascended into heaven, some of his apostles still doubted, just as Thomas had doubted (John 20:24–25). They could not believe that their Lord had truly risen from the dead. Matthew wrote, "But the eleven disciples went into Galilee, unto the mountain where Jesus had appointed them. And when they saw him, they worshipped him; but some doubted" (Matthew 28:16–17). It appears that Mary was the only person who believed everything Jesus told her, but she had good reason to believe, for she of all people knew who Jesus was and where he had come from, and who His true Father was.

Jesus was born into this world to become exactly like all other men with one exception—not only was he the Son of man and the Son of God, but he was also Almighty Jehovah God himself. John wrote:

In the beginning was the Word, and the Word was with God, and the Word was God. The same was in the beginning with God. All things were made through him; and without him was not anything made that hath been made. In him was life; and the life was the light of men. (John 1:1–4)

As the apostle John continued, he said it was God who became flesh. "And the Word became flesh, and dwelt among us (and we beheld his glory, glory as of the only begotten from the Father), full of grace and truth" (John 1:14). Jesus is Jehovah God, the Almighty, and in him as a Man dwelt all the fullness of God (Colossians 2:9). Jeremiah wrote:

> Woe unto the shepherds that destroy and scatter the sheep of my pasture! saith Jehovah. Therefore thus saith Jehovah, the God of Israel, against the shepherds that feed my people: Ye have scattered my flock, and driven them away, and have not visited them; behold, I will visit upon you the evil of your doings, saith Jehovah. And I will gather the remnant of my flock out of all the countries whither I have driven them, and will bring them again to their folds; and they shall be fruitful and multiply. And I will set up shepherds over them, who shall feed them; and they shall fear no more, nor be dismayed, neither shall any be lacking, saith Jehovah. Behold, the days come, saith Jehovah, that I will raise unto David a righteous Branch, and he shall reign as king and deal wisely, and shall execute justice and righteousness in the land. In his days Judah shall be saved, and Israel shall dwell safely; and this is his name whereby he shall be called: Jehovah our righteousness. (Jeremiah 23:1–6)

Jesus is also Mighty God and the Eternal Father (Father of eternity). Isaiah wrote of Jesus when he said:

> For unto us a child is born, unto us a son is given; and the government shall be upon his shoulder: and his name shall be called Wonderful, Counsellor, Mighty God, Everlasting Father, Prince of

Peace. Of the increase of his government and of peace there shall be no end, upon the throne of David, and upon his kingdom, to establish it, and to uphold it with justice and with righteousness from henceforth even for ever. The zeal of Jehovah of hosts will perform this. (Isaiah 9:6–7)

Jesus left heaven, his throne of glory, and his unapproachable light when he came into the world to become a man like all other men. He came to take away the sins of the world. But Jesus was no ordinary man. He was the Almighty Jehovah God himself who was willing to give up his equality with God to become a man—a man who in all points was just like all other men (Hebrews 2:17). It was God who was willing to give up his glory, his power, and his authority as the Almighty to become our Savior—but he never gave up his deity. Paul wrote:

Have this mind in you, which was also in Christ Jesus: who, existing in the form of God, counted not the being on an equality with God a thing to be grasped, but emptied himself, taking the form of a servant, being made in the likeness of men; and being found in fashion as a man, he humbled himself, becoming obedient even unto death, yea, the death of the cross. (Philippians 2:5–8)

What a sacrifice the Word was willing to make when he was prepared to give up everything that made him equal to God and become a man in all points like all other men. Not only did Jesus become a man, but he also became the poorest of the poor of all men. One day when Jesus and Peter were asked to pay a half-shekel temple tax, which is very close to nothing, neither Jesus nor Peter had that much money between them. Jesus told Peter to go fishing, and he would find the money they needed in a fish's mouth (Matthew 17:24–27).

When Jesus was crucified his only possession was the garment he was wearing. The Roman soldiers who crucified him cast lots to see which one of them would possess it after Jesus had died. Jesus' mother was probably the one who made that garment for him, and she had to witness the soldiers gambling over it.

Jesus was willing to take all the abuse that other men would subject him to. He was prepared to be spit on, mocked, scourged, beaten, crowned with thorns, and killed by being nailed to a cross (Matthew 27:27–31)—*and left to die alone*—he was even forsaken by God when he died! (Mathew 27:46).

If the king of a province lost one of his men and he received a ransom note from his captors demanding that it be paid or he would never see that man again, the king would have to consider if the man were worth the ransom, and how much should be paid. But if the man who was captured was the king's son the ransom would be paid no matter how much it cost. So also it was with God and his Son—and the value of the creation. God considered his Son to be of considerably more value than the entire world he had created. Therefore, when Jesus offered himself as the ransom that was demanded to redeem the creation from the corruption of Adam's sin, and all sin, he was paying a price that was much greater than was required. The value of Jesus—*and his cross*—was much greater than what was necessary to make full compensation for all the damage Adam's sin had caused, and to pay the price necessary to restore all things back into their original perfection and beauty—and abolish death (2 Timothy 1:10).

In the Old Testament there was no Son of God, but Jesus has always been the Word (John 1:1). When the Word was born to a virgin to become the Son of God and the Son of man, he truly became a man just like all other men. The writer of Hebrews wrote of Jesus when he became the Son of man, and he said:

But we behold him who hath been made a little lower than the angels, even Jesus, because of the suffering of death crowned with glory and honor, that by the grace of God he should taste of death for every man. For it became him, for whom are all things, and through whom are all things, in bringing many sons unto glory, to make the author of their salvation perfect through sufferings. For both he that sanctifieth and they that are sanctified are all of one: for which cause he is not ashamed to call them brethren, saying, I will declare thy name unto my brethren, In the midst of the congregation will I sing thy praise. And again, I will put my trust in him. And again, Behold, I and the children whom God hath given me. Since then the children are sharers in flesh and blood, he also himself in like manner partook of the same; that through death he might bring to nought him that had the power of death, that is, the devil; and might deliver all them who through fear of death were all their lifetime subject to bondage. For verily not to angels doth he give help, but he giveth help to the seed of Abraham. Wherefore it behooved him in all things to be made like unto his brethren, that he might become a merciful and faithful high priest in things pertaining to God, to make propitiation for the sins of the people. For in that he himself hath suffered being tempted, he is able to succor them that are tempted. (Hebrews 2:9–18)

Jesus had no advantages over other men whatsoever—not in any fashion. He had given up his equality, his power, his authority, and his glory as God, and he had to trust his Father for all that he accomplished—and that included his power to work miracles. Jesus had to live by faith just as we must live by faith (Hebrews 2:11-13). Every miracle that Jesus accomplished was achieved by the power of his Father working in him rather than by Jesus himself. Jesus confirmed that when he said:

> I can of myself do nothing: as I hear, I judge: and my judgment is righteous; because I seek not mine own will, but the will of him that sent me. (John 5.30)

> Jesus therefore answered and said unto them, Verily, verily, I say unto you, The Son can do nothing of himself, but what he seeth the Father doing: for what things soever he doeth, these the Son also doeth in like manner. (John 5:19)

> Jesus therefore said, When ye have lifted up the Son of man, then shall ye know that I AM, and that I do nothing of myself, but as the Father taught me, I speak these things. And he that sent me is with me; he hath not left me alone; for I do always the things that are pleasing to him. As he spake these things, many believed on him. (John 8:28–30)

Jesus was tempted in all points just like all other men are tempted. He knew what it was like to suffer such extreme overpowering temptation that it seemed impossible to endure it. However, he did endure it, and he expects us to do the same (1Corinthians 10:12-13). The writer of Hebrews said:

> Having then a great high priest, who hath passed through the heavens, Jesus the Son of God, let us

hold fast our confession. For we have not a high priest that cannot be touched with the feeling of our infirmities; but one that hath been in all points tempted like as we are, yet without sin. Let us therefore draw near with boldness unto the throne of grace, that we may receive mercy, and may find grace to help us in time of need. (Hebrews 4:14–16)

I believe Jesus was tempted much more severely than any other man has ever been tempted. Jesus is God, but there were occasions when as the Son of Man he was tempted brutally—like the time the Holy Spirit led him into the wilderness to be tempted by Satan for forty days, and forty nights (Luke 4:1-13). Another time is when he was in the garden praying to his Father that he would not have to drink the cup (that is, to have to go to the cross). Jesus himself had a way out of that garden, and he had a way out of going to the cross—if he wanted to use it. He could have called upon the power of his own deity to escape the cross and just walk right out of that garden. Had he chosen to do he would have saved himself, but his entire creation and everyone in it would have been faced with death and annihilation. Also, all the saints in the Old Testament who had been forgiven of their sins would once again be held accountable for their transgressions. The animal sacrifices they offered to have their sins forgiven did not pardon their trespasses (Hebrews 10:1–4). Also, all the promises of God concerning the salvation of his creation and the restoration of all things (Acts 3:21) would have failed. The Almighty's promise to Abraham that he would become the father of a mighty nation (Genesis 12:2–3, 17:1–9), and that through him all the nations of the world would be blessed, (Galatians 3:6–9) would also have failed.

When we are tempted, there are two things we should remember that will aid us in overcoming all temptations. We should use

149

them both as our strength to overcome every unbearable entice-
ment, and not give into it by sinning. Once a person yields to
temptation, the temptation is gone, but that results in sin (James
1:13-16). First: we shall never be tempted beyond what we are
able to endure, for there is always a means of escape from any
temptation. Paul wrote:

> There hath no temptation taken you but such as
> man can bear: but God is faithful, who will not
> suffer you to be tempted above that ye are able;
> but will with the temptation make also the way of
> escape, that ye may be able to endure it. (1 Cor-
> inthians 10:13)

The other thing we should remember is how Jesus handled his
temptation when he was in the garden, and he fervently prayed
to his Father that he might not have to drink the cup—that is, to
not have to go to the cross. He never yielded to that temptation
by avoiding the cross; rather he gave in to his Father's will when
he said: "My Father, if this cannot pass away, except I drink it,
thy will be done" (Matthew 26:42). The Father's will is always
best no matter how strongly we want something else, even if it
is contrary to his will. Sometimes we feel that our Father's will
is just a little too severe—such as the way Jesus must have felt in
the garden—and therefore we look for another way, when there
is no other way. Matthew wrote of Jesus' suffering and his great
temptation when he wrote:

> Then cometh Jesus with them unto a place called
> Gethsemane, and saith unto his disciples, Sit ye
> here, while I go yonder and pray. And he took with
> him Peter and the two sons of Zebedee, and be-
> gan to be sorrowful and sore troubled. Then saith
> he unto them, My soul is exceeding sorrowful,

even unto death: abide ye here, and watch with me. And he went forward a little, and fell on his face, and prayed, saying, My Father, if it be possible, let this cup pass away from me: nevertheless, not as I will, but as thou wilt. And he cometh unto the disciples, and findeth them sleeping, and saith unto Peter, What, could ye not watch with me one hour? Watch and pray, that ye enter not into temptation: the spirit indeed is willing, but the flesh is weak. Again a second time he went away, and prayed, saying, My Father, if this cannot pass away, except I drink it, thy will be done. And he came again and found them sleeping, for their eyes were heavy. And he left them again, and went away, and prayed a third time, saying again the same words. Then cometh he to the disciples, and saith unto them, Sleep on now, and take your rest: behold, the hour is at hand, and the Son of man is betrayed into the hands of sinners. Arise, let us be going: behold, he is at hand that betrayeth me. (Matthew 26:36–46)

Luke also gave an account of how Jesus suffered such severe temptation that it appears to have been just as painful as when he was actually being nailed to the cross. Luke wrote:

And he came out, and went, as his custom was, unto the mount of Olives; and the disciples also followed him. And when he was at the place, he said unto them, Pray that ye enter not into temptation. And he was parted from them about a stone's cast; and he kneeled down and prayed, saying, Father, if thou be willing, remove this cup from me: nevertheless not my will, but thine, be done. And there appeared unto him an angel from heaven, strengthening him. And being in an agony he prayed more earnestly; and his sweat became as it were great drops of blood falling down upon the ground. (Luke 22:39–44)

What we are viewing in these Scriptures is the price the Almighty was willing to pay to forgive Adam's sin, to redeem his creation, to take away all the sins of the world (John 1:29)

—and set all men free from sin and death—it was his own Son's blood. The Father paid that price by offering his Son as a sacrifice on a cross, and it was that sacrifice that gave God's children his holiness, his righteousness, and eternal life. The price the Son paid was to be spit on, scourged, humiliated, mocked, beaten with many stripes, crowned with thorns, and put to death by being nailed to a cross (Matthew 27:27–44). Even with all the power and majesty God has there was no other way that the salvation of God's children, and the restoration of all things, could have been accomplished.

This might be an interesting question: When Jesus was suffering in the garden and pleading with his Father to not have to drink the cup of the cross; and when he was about to die on the cross and cried, "Eli, Eli, lama sabachthani? (that is, My God, my God, why hast thou forsaken me?")—who suffered the most? Was it the Son who was in actual pain, or was it the Father who had to witness his own beloved Son suffer such things? There are many men and women who would die for another person, such as their children, their mate, or a brother—or maybe a very close and dear friend. But who would allow their child to die for the sake of anyone or anything? Who would sacrifice their only child to save their very worst enemy? That is exactly what God our Father did for us. Paul wrote:

For while we were yet weak, in due season Christ died for the ungodly. For scarcely for a righteous man will one die: for peradventure for the good man some one would even dare to die. But God commendeth his own love toward us, in that, while we were yet sinners, Christ died for us. Much more then, being now justified by his blood, shall we be saved from the wrath of God through him. For if, while we were enemies, we were reconciled to God through the death of his Son, much more, being reconciled, shall we be saved by his life. (Romans 5:6-10)

The Father knew full well that he could stop Jesus' suffering in a moment of time, but he also knew the redemption of the creation, the restoration of all things, the salvation of all his children—and all his promises being fulfilled—depended on that cross being and accomplished fact. That could only be achieved by the death of the one who was nailed to it.

What Jesus was willing to give up in becoming our Savior was a very costly sacrifice. He was willing to give up his equality with God and become a man in all points just like other men, and then to be treated very shamefully. But after Jesus' resurrection that all changed. After Jesus' was raised from the dead God gave him back everything he had given up to become a Man—and that Man had the power and the authority to redeem all other men and set them free from sin and death. Jesus accomplished that by his sinless life, his cross, and his resurrection. Because of his great achievement he was rewarded with all the honor, the glory, the authority, and the power that the Almighty Jehovah God himself has—Jesus, as a Man, was made in all points equal to God, and he was made the King of kings and the Lord of lords (Revelation 17:14).

Just before Jesus left this world in his human body and ascended into the heavens, he called his apostles together for their
last commands:

> But the eleven disciples went into Galilee, unto
> the mountain where Jesus had appointed them.
> And when they saw him, they worshipped him;
> but some doubted. And Jesus came to them and
> spake unto them, saying, All authority hath been
> given unto me in heaven and on earth. Go ye
> therefore, and make disciples of all the nations,
> baptizing them into the name of the Father and of
> the Son and of the Holy Spirit: teaching them to
> observe all things whatsoever I commanded you:
> and lo, I am with you always, even unto the end of
> the world. (Matthew 28:16–20)

Just before Jesus ascended into heaven God gave him all authority on earth and in heaven, and there is no more power and
no more authority anywhere else that existed: Jesus had it all. It
is the Man, Jesus, who is King over the entire creation, in heav-
en and on this earth, and he shall rule as the Son of man until
he comes again. After the judgment, and after the new heavens
and the new earth have been established, Jesus shall be restored
back into the Godhead as Almighty Jehovah God himself (1
Corinthians 15:21-28) —then he will be the same One he had
been before he became the Son of man. Jesus is to this day is still
a Man, but he is a spiritual man in a spiritual body. He is the Man
who shall be our Judge. Luke wrote:

> The times of ignorance therefore God over-
> looked; but now he commandeth men that they
> should all everywhere repent: inasmuch as he
> hath appointed a day in which he will judge the

world in righteousness by the man whom he hath ordained; whereof he hath given assurance unto all men, in that he hath raised him from the dead. (Acts 17:30–31)

John wrote:

For neither doth the Father judge any man, but he hath given all judgment unto the Son; that all may honor the Son, even as they honor the Father. He that honoreth not the Son honoreth not the Father that sent him. (John 5:22–23)

The reason the Father gave all judgment to the Son is because Jesus had been a man in all points like other men. Jesus knows, by experience, how difficult it is to live in this present evil world and just survive, let alone live without sin. But he did exactly that. Therefore, Jesus shall be our Judge because he can judge us fairly, and so we can be assured that we have been judged fairly, for he has been one of us; he has walked in our shoes, and he knows about all our struggles. John wrote, "For as the Father hath life in himself, even so gave he to the Son also to have life in himself: and he gave him authority to execute judgment, because he is a son of man" (John 5:26–27).

To further illustrate that Jesus is still the Man who rules over all things, and that he rules by the delegated authority his Father gave him, we shall view what Paul wrote. Paul said that Jesus must be a Man for him to be our Mediator, and to fulfill that assignment he must also be God:

This is good and acceptable in the sight of God our Saviour; who would have all men to be saved, and come to the knowledge of the truth. For there is one God, one mediator also between God and

men, himself man, Christ Jesus, who gave himself
a ransom for all; the testimony to be borne in its
own times. (1 Timothy 2:3–6)

The writer of Hebrews said that for Jesus to become our High
Priest he had to be a man, and he had to be taken from among
men to fill that position:

> For every high priest, being taken from among
> men, is appointed for men in things pertaining to
> God, that he may offer both gifts and sacrifices
> for sins: who can bear gently with the ignorant
> and erring, for that he himself also is compassed
> with infirmity; and by reason thereof is bound,
> as for the people, so also for himself, to offer for
> sins. And no man taketh the honor unto himself,
> but when he is called of God, even as was Aaron.
> So Christ also glorified not himself to be made a
> high priest, but he that spake unto him, thou art
> my Son, This day have I begotten thee: as he saith
> also in another place, Thou art a priest for ever
> After the order of Melchizedek. (Hebrews 5:1–6)

When this age comes to an end, and this present evil world
perishes in intense fire, and the new heavens and the new earth
appear ("wherein dwelleth righteousness") (2 Peter 3:10–13),
Jesus shall no longer be the Son of man and the Son of God. At
that time Jesus shall return to the Godhead as Almighty Jehovah
God himself exactly as he was before he became the Son of Man.
Paul wrote:

> Then cometh the end, when he shall deliver up
> the kingdom to God, even the Father; when he
> shall have abolished all rule and all authority and

power. For he must reign, till he hath put all his enemies under his feet. The last enemy that shall be abolished is death. For, He put all things in subjection under his feet. But when he saith, All things are put in subjection, it is evident that he is excepted who did subject all things unto him. And when all things have been subjected unto him, then shall the Son also himself be subjected to him that did subject all things unto him, that God may be all in all. (1 Corinthians 15:24–28)

When Jesus became the Son of man and died, and was resurrected, after his resurrection the Father subjected all things into his hands (that is, all things except the Father himself). That was all given to Jesus as a Man, and it was his reward for the tremendous task he had accomplished with his cross. When this age ends and the new heavens and the new earth are established, Jesus will enter back into the Godhead as he was before he became the Son of Man, and it will be Jesus, the Man, who subjects all the things back to the Father, all the things the Father had subjected unto him. Jesus shall also subject himself as the Son of man back into the hands of his Father, and he shall deliver the kingdom he established with his cross up to his Father. That kingdom is the church. That is also the time when all rule, authority, and power shall be abolished (that is, all the rule, authority, and power that does not inherently belong to God) —and that includes the authority that God gave Jesus the day he ascended from the mount into heaven (Matthew 28:17–20). When that transpires the only rule, power, and authority that shall exist is that which inherently belongs to God. That shall begin the time when Jesus shall rule over all things along with the Father and the Holy Spirit—but Jesus shall rule by his own authority as God, and not by the delegated authority that had been given to him as the Son of God and the Son of man.

This should bring us to the point where we can see how one Man could annul Adam's sin and deliver all men from its consequences—that was all possible because of the value of the One who came to accomplish it; He was Almighty Jehovah God himself in a human body; He was God's only begotten Son whom God loved dearly.

We have answered with a logical view the reason God condemned the world and everyone in it to death because of the sin of one man—it was who that man was, and what he did. We have also seen that it was not an unrighteous act for God to condemn the entire human population for the sin of one man, because that condemnation never fell upon anyone, except Jesus. Jesus, who is God, took the whole burden of all sin upon himself, and he paid for it in full with his cross, and that maintained the righteous of God in everything he did.

I believe we have also answered the question regarding how the death of another Man, who is Jesus, could annul the consequences of the terrible act of disobedience that was committed by his brother, Adam; and why he had the power to restore the creation back to its original perfection, beauty, and glory. It was because of who that man was—God's only begotten Son—and what he accomplished with his perfect life. It was by that Man's holy act of righteous obedience that he abolished the condemnation Adam caused by his unholy act of disobedience. But that isn't all: The cross not only annulled the death that Adam caused to fall upon all men; it also offers the forgiveness of sin to each individual person who has transgressed the commandments of God himself (resulting in sin). With the forgiveness of sin comes the promise of the free gift of eternal life to all who would obey God's simple command, "He that believeth and is baptized shall be saved; but he that disbelieveth shall be condemned" (Mark 16:16).

CHAPTER 5

❃

THE PRICE GOD PAID TO ABOLISH

DEATH AND RESTORE HIS CREATION—

THE THREE DAYS OF THE CROSS

TO UNDERSTAND THE PRICE God paid, how unbearably he was willing to suffer, and what he was willing to give up and endure to save his creation, we must go back to the time of Moses. Moses was one of God's most trusted servants (Numbers 12:7–8). He served God faithfully throughout his entire life of 120 years. He served in the palace of Pharaoh, in Egypt, for forty years as the adopted son of Pharaoh's daughter, but it was his birth mother who was his teacher and nursemaid, and she was the one who actually raised Moses (Exodus 2:1–10). During that time Moses learned the Egyptian language, the Egyptian ways, and the Egyptian culture—and he learned how to deal with Pharaoh. He also learned from his mother that he was an Israelite, and not an Egyptian, and that he was the chosen one who would deliver his people, Israel, out of Egyptian bondage. When Moses tried that on his own initiative he made a terrible mistake, and he was forced to leave Egypt and live in the desert (Exodus 2:10–15). Moses lived in the desert for forty years learning how to survive in the wilderness, just like it was his home, because for the next eighty years it would be his home.

Moses spent the last forty years of his life leading the children of Israel through the desert wilderness and into the land God had promised them. Without his experience in living in the wilderness for forty years, that would have been very difficult— maybe impossible. But those last forty years were the most challenging time of his entire life. God is not limited, but Moses was the only man in the world who was qualified to lead Israel, the nation of God's children, out of Egyptian bondage and into their promised land. Forty years living in Pharoah's palace, and forty years living in the wilderness is what qualified him.

One day when Moses was tending to his business, he saw a bush that was on fire, but the bush was not consumed by the flames. When Moses went to the bush he heard a voice, "Moses, take off your shoes, you are standing on holy ground! (Exodus 3:1-5). The voice was from Almighty God, and it was that moment he became known as Israel's covenant God, and he would from that day on be known by his covenant name, the great *I AM*, who is Jehovah (Exodus 3:14). He told Moses to return to Egypt and deliver his people, Israel, from their bondage to Pharoah. Moses said he had tried that many years ago, and it didn't work, he just got into great trouble, *"I am not going!"* God said, *"We shall see about that!"* Moses went.

It was during that time after many years of very hard service that Moses wanted to know who he was serving—He could hear the voice guiding him, and he understood it, but he saw no person. So, Moses asked the Almighty, "Who are you? —I want to see you!" God's response was, "No man shall see my face and live!" (Exodus 33:17–23). Not even Moses, with whom God spoke mouth to mouth, or face to face (Numbers 12:5–8) could see the face of God and live.

From this we can see what God gave up and the price he paid to restore his creation from its fallen state back to its original glory and perfection. We can also see the value of the free gift that Jesus offers to all men: the forgiveness of sin, and eternal life to all who will believe and obey. God left his Holy Place and his throne of glory, where not even an angel could approach his presence without being invited, to become a man just like all other men (Hebrews 2:17). As a man he was seen in person by many men, even sinners, and anyone who looked into the eyes of Jesus were looking into the face of Almighty Jehovah God himself. Phillip, one of Jesus' apostles, wanted to see the Father, just as Moses wanted to see him, and this was Jesus' response:

> Jesus saith unto him, I am the way, and the truth, and the life: no one cometh unto the Father, but by me. If ye had known me, ye would have known my Father also: from henceforth ye know him, and have seen him. Philip saith unto him, Lord, show us the Father, and it sufficeth us. Jesus saith unto him, Have I been so long time with you, and dost thou not know me, Philip? he that hath seen me hath seen the Father; how sayest thou, Show us the Father? Believest thou not that I am in the Father, and the Father in me? the words that I say unto you I speak not from myself: but the Father abiding in me doeth his works. Believe me that I am in the Father, and the Father in me: or else believe me for the very works' sake. (John 14:6–11)

The day is coming when all of God's children shall see their Father, and Jesus his Son, in all the fullness of their glory and beauty. What is so amazing about that day is when the sons of God view their Father and His Son, the Almighty God in all his glory, they shall be just like him, and they shall live with him forever. John wrote:

> Behold what manner of love the Father hath bestowed upon us, that we should be called children of God; and such we are. For this cause the world knoweth us not, because it knew him not. Beloved, now are we children of God, and it is not yet made manifest what we shall be. We know that, if he shall be manifested, we shall be like him; for we shall see him even as he is. And every one that hath this hope set on him purifieth himself, even as he is pure" (1 John 1:1–3)

It was the infinite Almighty One—he who would allow no one to see his face and live— who was willing to give up his throne of glory to become a man who could be seen by everyone. He was also willing to give up his equality with God to become that Man (Philippians 2:5–8). Now, let us consider the price God was willing to pay to redeem his creation from its fallen state and offer the free gift of eternal life to all men. With that free gift of life comes the gift of God's own holiness (1 Peter 1:15–16), and the gift his own righteousness (2 Corinthians 5:21; 1 John 3:6–7) to all who would believe him and obey him. So, what ransom was Jesus willing to pay (Matthew 20:28; 1 Timothy 2:5–6) to accomplish that and take away the sins of the world? We need to read what Matthew wrote to understand what the Father was willing to allow his Son to endure, and what Jesus was willing to suffer, so that we might be saved from sin and death and receive free gift of eternal life:

> Pilate saith unto them, What then shall I do unto Jesus who is called Christ? They all say, Let him be crucified. And he said, Why, what evil hath

he done? But they cried out exceedingly, saying, Let him be crucified. So when Pilate saw that he prevailed nothing, but rather that a tumult was arising, he took water, and washed his hands before the multitude, saying, I am innocent of the blood of this righteous man; see ye to it. And all the people answered and said, His blood be on us, and on our children. Then released he unto them Barabbas; but Jesus he scourged and delivered to be crucified. Then the soldiers of the governor took Jesus into the Praetorium, and gathered unto him the whole band. And they stripped him, and put on him a scarlet robe. And they platted a crown of thorns and put it upon his head, and a reed in his right hand; and they kneeled down before him, and mocked him, saying, Hail, King of the Jews! And they spat upon him, and took the reed and smote him on the head. And when they had mocked him, they took off from him the robe, and put on him his garments, and led him away to crucify him. And as they came out, they found a man of Cyrene, Simon by name: him they compelled to go with them, that he might bear his cross. And they were come unto a place called Golgotha, that is to say, The place of a skull, they gave him wine to drink mingled with gall: and when he had tasted it, he would not drink. And when they had crucified him, they parted his garments among them, casting lots; and they sat and watched him there. And they set up over his head his accusation written, THIS IS JESUS THE KING OF THE JEWS. Then are there crucified with him two robbers, one on the right hand and one on the left. And they that passed by railed on him, wagging their heads, and saying, Thou that destroyest the temple, and buildest it in three days, save thyself: if thou art the Son of God, come down from the cross. In like manner also the chief priests mocking him, with the scribes and elders, said, He saved others; himself he cannot save. He is the King of Israel; let him now come down from the cross, and we will believe on him. He trusteth on God; let him deliver him now, if he desireth him: for he said, I am the Son of God. And the robbers also that were crucified with him cast upon him the same reproach. (Matthew 27:22–44)

It is impossible to even imagine why the Most Holy One (who was so holy that he would not permit anyone to see his face and live) would allow himself to be put into such a position as Matthew described. The physical sufferings and death that Jesus was willing to endure were only part of his torment. It was the spiritual suffering and death that Jesus dreaded the most. That was the cup Jesus prayed he would not have to drink when he was praying to his Father in the garden (Matthew 26:36–44). It was Jesus' spiritual death that caused him the most pain and suffering, because when Jesus drank that cup, he was separated from God, he was made to be sin (2 Corinthians 5:21), and he was cut off out of the land of the living (Isaiah 53:8). He who is the Way, the Truth, and the Life, and the giver of all life was himself cut off out of the land of the living. It is not possible for us to even begin to understand the pain, the suffering, the anxiety, and the grief that Jesus suffered when he made that pitiful cry from the cross: "And about the ninth hour Jesus cried with a loud voice, saying, Eli, Eli, lama sabachthani? that is, My God, my God, why hast thou forsaken me?" (Matthew 27:46). That was such a horrible experience for Jesus, and the Father, that it is far beyond description. Isaiah wrote:

He was oppressed, yet when he was afflicted he opened not his mouth; as a lamb that is led to the slaughter, and as a sheep that before its shearers is dumb, so he opened not his mouth. By oppression and judgment he was taken away; and as for his generation, who among them considered that he was cut off out of the land of the living for the transgression of my people to whom the stroke was due? (Isaiah 53:7–8)

The time when Jesus made that pitiful cry from the cross was the moment he poured out his soul unto death, and God made his soul an offering for sin. That is when God saw the travail of his soul and was satisfied. Isaiah 53:10–11 says:

Yet it pleased Jehovah to bruise him; he hath put him to grief: when thou shalt make his soul an offering for sin, he shall see his seed, he shall prolong his days, and the pleasure of Jehovah shall prosper in his hand. He shall see of the travail of his soul, and shall be satisfied: by the knowledge of himself shall my righteous servant justify many; and he shall bear their iniquities.

And that brings us to the three days of the cross. The day of the cross was the most tragic day, and yet it was the most glorious day in the history of God's creation. It was tragic because an innocent man was crucified for being whom he claimed to be. Jesus was crucified for claiming to be the Son of God (John 5:18, 10:30–33), and the King of Israel (John 18:33-38), and truly he was. He came to tell us about his Father, and his Father's love for all men. He came to teach all men that by believing in the Father and his Son they would have the forgiveness of sin, and they would be given the gift of eternal life (John 3:14–18; 5:24;

17:3). For teaching those things he was crucified (John 8:51–59; 10:27–33).

The day of the cross was the very special day that the Father had planned before the foundation of the world—it was the day in which all sin was punished and abolished forever, and when all men were forgiven of all sin (Luke 23:34) and set free from sin, law, and death. Sin is never forgiven; it is always punished— It is always the sinner who is forgiven. It was on the day of the cross that all sins received their just recompense and were punished, while the sinners were forgiven and set free (Galatians 5:1). But men receive that wonderful free gift only when they believe in Jesus, repent from their past way of living, and turn to God for forgiveness. That is all accomplished by faith. Hebrews 11:6 says, "And without faith it is impossible to be well-pleasing unto him; for he that cometh to God must believe that he is, and that he is a rewarder of them that seek after him."

There have been times when God's wrath was strongly poured out against sin and rebellion, but never has God's wrath been vented against sin in any greater measure than it was expressed on the day of the cross. It was about 1656 years after God created the world that his wrath and anger against violence and evil were very strongly vented upon all mankind, because all men had become very wicked indeed. Genesis 6:5–7 says:

> And Jehovah saw that the wickedness of man was great in the earth, and that every imagination of the thoughts of his heart was only evil continually. And it repented Jehovah that he had made man on the earth, and it grieved him at his heart. And Jehovah said, I will destroy man whom I have created from the face of the ground; both man, and beast, and creeping things, and birds of the heavens; for it repenteth me that I have made them.

Only Noah was found to be righteous, and he and his family were spared from the great flood that covered the entire earth and destroyed all living creatures (Genesis 7:23; 2 Peter 2:4–5).

There was another occasion when God's wrath fell so very heavily on sinful men that it destroyed their cities. That was the day God destroyed Sodom and Gomorrah, the five cities of the plains (Genesis 18:20; 19:23–25). Peter said God's anger was so strong against those cities that he turned them into ashes. Peter wrote, 2 Peter 2:6: "And turning the cities of Sodom and Gomorrah into ashes condemned them with an overthrow, having made them an example unto those that should live ungodly." I have read about the works of scientists who have excavated the area where Sodom and Gomorrah used to be, and they said that they found gold there that had been crystalized. It takes six thousand degrees Fahrenheit to crystalize gold, and that is hotter than the surface of the sun! The Almighty must have been quite angry!

But never has God's wrath been vented in any stronger measure against sin and rebellion than it was on the day Jesus died on the cross. It was that day God punished sin—all sin—once, for all, and forever. That was the day God dealt with all the problems and devastation that sin had caused, and it was Jesus who took God's wrath upon himself and paid the price God demanded in full so that all sinners could be forgiven. It is not even possible to describe, or even imagine the magnificence and the greatness of that kind of love. Matthew and Luke both described the day Jesus died on the cross vividly:

> Now from the sixth hour there was darkness over all the land until the ninth hour. And about the ninth hour Jesus cried with a loud voice, saying, Eli, Eli, lama sabachthani? that is, My God, my God, why hast thou forsaken me? And some of them stood there, when they heard it, said, This

man calleth Elijah. And straightway one of them ran, and took a sponge, and filled it with vinegar, and put it on a reed, and gave him to drink. And the rest said, Let be; let us see whether Elijah cometh to save him. And Jesus cried again with a loud voice, and yielded up his spirit. And behold, the veil of the temple was rent in two from the top to the bottom; and the earth did quake; and the rocks were rent; and the tombs were opened; and many bodies of the saints that had fallen asleep were raised. (Matthew 27:45–52)

And it was now about the sixth hour, and a darkness came over the whole land until the ninth hour, the sun's light failing: and the veil of the temple was rent in the midst. And Jesus, crying with a loud voice, said, Father, into thy hands I commend my spirit: and having said this, he gave up the ghost. And when the centurion saw what was done, he glorified God, saying, Certainly this was a righteous man. And all the multitudes that came together to this sight, when they beheld the things that were done, returned smiting their breasts. (Luke 23:44–48)

It was not those who were crucifying Jesus who were the object of God's wrath because they were crucifying his Son. It was the one who was nailed to the cross and dying, God's own Son, who was suffering the pain of God's wrath. God was punishing sin, and it was Jesus who was taking that punishment upon himself, because he had been made to be sin (2 Corinthians 5:21). The punishment that should have fallen upon Adam and other men who had committed the terrible acts of aggression against the Father (the very trespasses for which Jesus was paying the price to correct, Isaiah 53:4–8); all fell upon Jesus.

Jesus was made to be sin for us so we could be saved and made to be righteous. Second Corinthians 5:21 says, "Him who knew no sin he made to be sin on our behalf; that we might become the righteousness of God in him." John wrote, "My little children, let no man lead you astray: he that doeth righteousness is righteous, even as he is righteous" (1 John 3:7). What Jesus was willing to suffer for us, and the punishment he was willing to take upon himself for our sins, is beyond our greatest imagination. What God hated most—sin—is what he actually became for us in his Son so we might be delivered from sin and its penalty, which is death—and so we might be made as righteous as God himself is righteous (2 Corinthians 5:21; 1 John 3:7). All of that was accomplished by the way of the cross. That is how much love God has for us. Paul wrote:

> For while we were yet weak, in due season Christ died for the ungodly. For scarcely for a righteous man will one die: for peradventure for the good man some one would even dare to die. But God commendeth his own love toward us, in that, while we were yet sinners, Christ died for us. Much more then, being now justified by his blood, shall we be saved from the wrath of God through him. For if, while we were enemies, we were reconciled to God through the death of his Son, much more, being reconciled, shall we be saved by his life; and not only so, but we also rejoice in God through our Lord Jesus Christ, through whom we have now received the reconciliation. (Romans 5:6–11)

When we view the day of the cross, the very day when Jesus was crucified, we can understand many things about God and his Son, Jesus. For instance, we can truly see we serve a very humble but mighty God. He is the Almighty, but he is full of humility, love, grace, mercy, and peace, for God is love (1 John 4:8, 16). Humility is not a sign of weakness; it is a sign of power and self-control. When Jesus was on the cross and they were driving the nails into his hands and feet, Jesus' concern was for those who were crucifying him and committing such an appalling and unspeakable act of violence. Jesus said, "Father, forgive them; for they know not what they do. And parting his garments among them, they cast lots" (Luke 23:34). Truly casting lots for his garment while they were nailing him to the cross is a clear example of heaping insult upon injury, but this illustrates how Jesus lived; he was always more concerned about others than he was for himself.

There is something else we can understand about God from the day that Jesus was crucified. We can see the magnitude of God's love, his grace, and his mercy. When Jesus was hanging on the cross and in terrible pain, both physically and spiritually, all the people who were there witnessing that event were insulting him, and mocking him, except for his mother and one or two of his disciples. Even the thieves who were dying with him were mocking him (Matthew 27:44). Jesus, in his quiet and controlled manner ignored it all. But toward the end of the crucifixion when the three men on their crosses were about to die, two of them died quickly by having their legs broken so they could no longer breathe. Jesus died because his Father took him before that could be accomplished so the Scriptures would be fulfilled. The Scriptures prophesied that not a bone of the Lamb of God would be broken, and that all occurred exactly according to the Scriptures (Psalms 34:20; John 19:36).

One of the thieves who died with Jesus must have been a very intelligent and observing man. He had been with Jesus for several hours during the time of Jesus "*trial*," —and he noticed all the insults and maltreatment that had been heaped upon Jesus, and even he himself had joined in. Then he observed how Jesus responded to such abuse—Jesus just accepted it all and said nothing. Just before the three men died, with only minutes to live, one of the thieves came to the firm conclusion that Jesus was being crucified for claiming to be exactly who he was: the Son of God and the King of Israel. Luke wrote:

> And the people stood beholding. And the rulers also scoffed at him, saying, He saved others; let him save himself, if this is the Christ of God, his chosen. And the soldiers also mocked him, coming to him, offering him vinegar, and saying, If thou art the King of the Jews, save thyself. And there was also a superscription over him, THIS IS THE KING OF THE JEWS. And one of the malefactors that were hanged railed on him, saying, Art not thou the Christ? save thyself and us. But the other answered, and rebuking him said, Dost thou not even fear God, seeing thou art in the same condemnation? And we indeed justly; for we receive the due reward of our deeds: but this man hath done nothing amiss. And he said, Jesus, remember me when thou comest in thy kingdom. And he said unto him, Verily I say unto thee, Today shalt thou be with me in Paradise. (Luke 23:35–43)

Jesus' exchange with the dying thief clearly illustrates one of the greatest examples of faith that can be found in the Bible. For here we see a dying man who was in great pain, and who confessed that he was dying a death he deserved for his terrible acts of violence and disobedience (Luke 23:40–41), looking to another man who was dying with him, and asking that man to save him—after they had both died! How did that man grasp all of that in just the few hours he had been with Jesus and listening to all the charges that were pronounced against him? Why couldn't his disciples and the apostles grasp that when they had been with him for some three years? What an example this is to all believers—especially to those who at times feel they are not worthy to be saved because of how little they are able to accomplish for God, or how insignificant they truly were. Everyone who feels that way should remember this incident and know that they have as much to offer God as that thief had to offer in just the few moments before he died. That thief was saved by his faith, and that is the only way that anyone can be saved (Ephesians 2:8–9; 2 Timothy 1:9; Titus 3:3–5). When the thief was saved and entered the kingdom of God (Luke 23:43) he became just as loved, just as great, and just as important as anyone who was in the kingdom of heaven, and that includes Noah, Abraham, Moses, David, Peter, Paul, and Mary; or any of the apostles. No one is made great in God's kingdom because of the magnitude of their works or saved by their own works. We are all saved the same way, and that is by the grace of God through our faith (Ephesians 2:8–9; 2 Timothy 1:9; Titus 3:3–5). Everyone who enters the kingdom of heaven does so by the blood of Christ and what Christ did for them—not what they did for themselves or even what they did for God. We all enter the kingdom of God by the blood of Christ and our faith. There is a parable in Matthew that verifies this: Matthew 20:1–16. It is the parable of the laborers and the vineyard. The master of the vineyard (who is God) went out into the community to find workers for his vineyard (his kingdom, or his church). He was seeking any laborers who would labor for him for a wage—In the case of God and his workers the wage was the free gift of eternal life (Romans 6:23). The master of the vineyard agreed to a shilling a day with the laborers he first met early in the morning. Three hours later he found more workers and told them to go work in the vineyard and he would give them what was right. He did the same thing again about three hours later. When there was only an hour left in the day, he hired more workers and just told them to go, work in the vineyard, and they went. When it was time to pay the laborers, he paid the last he hired first, and he paid all the workers the same wage. Those who worked an hour or so were very happy. Those who had worked all day and had received what they agreed to work for murmured, for they had labored all day and those who had worked only an hour were paid the same. The master's reply was that he had paid them what was agreed, and he had the right to do with what was his as he chose to do it. The wage (or rather the free gift) laborers receive for working in God's kingdom is always the same for everyone: it is eternal life in a perfect world where there is no disease, no pain, no hunger, no poverty, no thirst, no disappointments, no sorrow—and no death. What could be added to that, and what more could be paid?

Even though all men who inherit eternal life in the kingdom of God are counted equal, there are men whom God has recognized as exceptional. Some of those men are mentioned by name in the Bible; they are Job, Daniel, Noah, Moses, Samuel, Elijah, and others (Ezekiel 14:13-20; Jeremiah 15:1; Matthew 17:1-4).

Not only was the thief who was dying on the cross an example of great faith, it clearly illustrates the magnitude of God's love, mercy, and grace; and for that we should all be greatly thankful. God was willing to forgive a man of his sins and give him eternal life when he had lived a terrible life of violence, stealing, and even murder. However, no man should ever live a life of negligence and self-service, not caring about God at all, and expect to be saved in the last few hours or days of their life. A person might just die unexpectedly and not be ready, and that is an attitude that God will not accept.

When Jesus died on the cross his body was taken down and buried in a new tomb where no man had ever been laid (John 19:40–42). There was a good reason for that. When the disciples went to the tomb to anoint Jesus' body, and it was gone, they did not have to count bodies to see if it was Jesus' body that was missing. When the women arrived at the tomb, the first thing they saw was that the stone had been rolled away from its entrance. They entered the tomb, and Jesus was not there. Nobody was there—except an angel. That stone was not rolled away so Jesus could escape: it had been rolled away so the women could enter the tomb and see that Jesus was not there (Luke 24:1–3).

Jesus' body was in the tomb three days. But where were his soul and his spirit while his body was in the grave? When Jesus died on the cross, he took the full punishment for all sin upon himself, both spiritually and physically. Jesus died the exact same death that a sinner would die if that sinner had died in their sins without their sins being forgiven. It was Adam who brought sin and death into the world, and to this day men die physically because of Adam's sin. Little babies die, but they have never sinned. Little babies suffer death because of Adam's transgression, just as all living things suffer death because of Adam's trespass. But men die spiritually for their own sins. Romans 6:23 says, "For the wages of sin is death; but the free gift of God is eternal life in Christ Jesus our Lord." Ezekiel 18:20 says, "The soul that sinneth, it shall die: the son shall not bear the iniquity of the father, neither shall the father bear the iniquity of the son; the righteousness of the righteous shall be upon him, and the wickedness of the wicked shall be upon him."

Death is a separation. Physical death is the separation of the spirit and the soul from the body (James 2:26). It is only the Holy Spirit who can determine the difference between the soul of a man, and the spirit of a man (Hebrews 4:12). Physical death takes place the moment the spirit leaves the body. Spiritual death, when the soul dies, is when it is separated from God because of sin. For Jesus to pay fully and completely for our sins he had to experience the death of a sinner, both physically and spiritually, though he had no sin himself (John 8:46; Hebrews 4:15). Therefore, Jesus' cry from the cross when he was dying, "My God My God, why have you forsaken me?" had a true and real meaning. God had forsaken him because he had been made to be sin so we could be made righteous. Paul wrote, "Him who knew no sin he made to be sin on our behalf; that we might become the righteousness of God in him" (2 Corinthians 5:21). When Jesus was made to be sin it was sin that was nailed to the cross, and when he died it was sin that died. When Jesus was forsaken of God, it was sin that was forsaken of God and punished. Jesus was willing to bear all the grief and pain that sin had caused by taking that burden upon himself so we could be saved. That is how much God loves us. But where did Jesus' spirit go when he was forsaken of God?

It is a shame that there are people who have been raised in a religious environment in which they are taught, "This is the way it is; this is the way it has always been; and this is the way it will always be—don't question it." Or, "I know that is what it says, but let me tell you what it means." We should read the Bible ourselves and arrive at our own conclusion as to what the scriptures teach, and then study with other people to compare notes. A person who has been raised under the aforementioned way of thinking will study the Bible to prove what they already believe rather than study the Bible diligently with the purpose of learning what it really teaches.

There are times when I come to a Scripture that is very difficult to understand, like Romans chapter 5 (2 Peter 3:15–16). Maybe the real meaning of what a Scripture plainly says is very clear, but something I don't really want to accept—because it either just does not seem reasonable, or it is against what I have been taught. But when it is very evident that a passage of

Scripture means exactly what it says, then that is the way we ought to accept it.

I think we always need to be ready and willing to change our way of thinking about how we *interpret* the Bible when we see there is the possibility that we might be wrong in our way of thinking. It is very good to study the Bible with other people— especially when we are viewing a very challenging part of the Bible that is very difficult to understand. But we need to be wary of anyone we study the Bible with when they tell us, in regard to a Scripture, "I know that is what it seems to say but that is not what it really means." We also need to be ready, willing, and able to stand fast for what we know to be the truth, and not change our way of thinking at all, unless we see a very good reason to do so. Jesus is Lord, and he died on the cross to save us from law, sin, and death, and that point is not debatable. To be able to study the Bible using that approach takes great wisdom, maturity, patience, and understanding.

When the King James Bible was translated into English, the words the translators used to compose our English Bible were chosen very carefully. There were many translators, about fifty-eight in all, and they were all experts in their field—the very best king James could find. Later, if by chance one of the words did not seem to be the exact word that should have been used, it took two-thirds of the translating committee to make the change. The American Standard Bible is the King James Version that has been revised, but it is not a new translation. The New American Standard Bible is a new translation of the American Standard Bible, and it calls the American Standard Version, "*THE ROCK.*" That is why I use the American Standard Version—I like Rocks!

When I am in a Bible class and a person makes the comment that a word they don't like is a *bad translation,* I just cringe. Do they know more about how the Bible should have been translated than the translators who translated it? And do they know the languages used in the original version equally well? I also feel uncomfortable when I read the Bible in class, and it has a perfectly obvious meaning, but because of personal reasons, prejudices, and preferences, a person changes the meaning to make it fit what they already believe, or what they want it to say.

I love to study the Bible with people who do not see the Bible the way I see it— especially when it is a passage of Scripture that is very difficult to understand. I feel there is always the possibility that I might be in the wrong, and that I might learn something from someone else's viewpoint. Giving thanks to God I have had that experience many times. Maybe we all need to have the attitude Paul said the church in Beroea had. Paul wrote:

> And the brethren immediately sent away Paul and Silas by night unto Beroea: who when they were come thither went into the synagogue of the Jews. Now these were more noble than those in Thessalonica, in that they received the word with all readiness of the mind, examining the Scriptures daily, whether these things were so. (Acts 17:10–11)

One of the areas in the Bible where there seems to be some disagreement is where Jesus was, and what he did the three days his body was in the tomb. There are some who are terribly offended at even the suggestion that when Jesus' Spirit left his body, he, of his own volition, went into Hades. However, the Bible is very clear, though very brief, about what happened those three days. Jesus said himself that he must spend three days and three nights in the heart of the earth. Jesus said:

> But he answered and said unto them, An evil and adulterous generation seeketh after a sign; and there shall no sign be given to it but the sign of Jonah the prophet: for as Jonah was three days and

> three nights in the belly of the whale; so shall the
> Son of man be three days and three nights in the
> heart of the earth. (Matthew 12:39–40)

What Jesus said means much more than just his body being in the tomb three days and three nights. It was not just Jonah's body that was in the belly of a whale—it was all of Jonah. Paul also spoke of this:

> But unto each one of us was the grace given ac-
> cording to the measure of the gift of Christ.
> Wherefore he saith, When he ascended on high,
> he led captivity captive, and gave gifts unto men.
> (Now this, He ascended, what is it but that he also
> descended into the lower parts of the earth? He
> that descended is the same also that ascended far
> above all the heavens, that he might fill all things).
> (Ephesians 4:7–10)

The same Jesus that ascended far above the heavens right into the presence of his Father, is the same Jesus that descended into the heart (or the lower part) of the earth. The lower part of the earth is the place where evil spirits were sent to be punished for rebellion against God (2 Peter 2:4; Jude 1:6). Psalms 63:8–10 says:

> My soul followeth hard after thee: Thy right hand
> upholdeth me. But those that seek my soul, to de-
> stroy it, Shall go into the lower parts of the earth.
> They shall be given over to the power of the
> sword: They shall be a portion for foxes.

Isaiah chapter 53 is a chapter in the Bible that describes the sacrifice of Jesus and the day of the cross very clearly. It says that when Jesus died he took all the grief, all the sin, all the guilt, all the punishment, all the agony, and all the pain that was going to fall upon sinners—upon himself—and he was smitten for the transgressions that other men had committed. That chapter of Isaiah describes Jesus' spiritual punishment, which was being cut off out of the land of the living and pouring out his soul unto death. Isaiah 53:4–12 says:

> Surely he hath borne our griefs, and carried our sorrows; yet we did esteem him stricken, smitten of God, and afflicted. But he was wounded for our transgressions, he was bruised for our iniquities; the chastisement of our peace was upon him; and with his stripes we are healed. All we like sheep have gone astray; we have turned every one to his own way; and Jehovah hath laid on him the iniquity of us all. He was oppressed, yet when he was afflicted he opened not his mouth; as a lamb that is led to the slaughter, and as a sheep that before its shearers is dumb, so he opened not his mouth. By oppression and judgment he was taken away; and as for his generation, who among them considered that he was cut off out of the land of the living for the transgression of my people to whom the stroke was due? And they made his grave with the wicked, and with a rich man in his death; although he had done no violence, neither was any deceit in his mouth. Yet it pleased Jehovah to bruise him; he hath put him to grief: when thou shalt make his soul an offering for sin, he shall see his seed, he shall prolong his days, and the pleasure of Jehovah shall prosper in his hand. He shall see of the travail of his soul, and shall be satisfied: by the knowledge of himself shall my

righteous servant justify many; and he shall bear their iniquities. Therefore will I divide him a portion with the great, and he shall divide the spoil with the strong; because he poured out his soul unto death, and was numbered with the transgressors: yet he bare the sin of many, and made intercession for the transgressors.

Where was Jesus when he was *"cut off out of the land of the living?"* Where was Jesus when he was numbered with the transgressors, the very people who had committed the acts of rebellion against his Father—the very transgressions for which he was suffering? Where was Jesus' soul when God saw the travail of his soul and was satisfied? Where was Jesus when he poured out his soul unto death, and his soul died? The people who had committed the terrible acts of rebellion were the very ones upon whom the stroke of death should have fallen, but instead that stroke fell upon Jesus. When Jesus was nailed to the cross and died, and his body was placed in the tomb—that was not Jesus being cut off from the land of the living. This world is not the land of the living (Galatians 1:4). Jesus was cut off out of the land of the living when he poured out his soul unto death (Isaiah 53:10–12). When Jesus died on the cross, his soul also died (Isaiah 53:12), his spirit was separated from God; and he was willing to suffer all of that for us. The land of the living is where God lives. Psalms 27:13 says, "I had fainted, unless I had believed to see the goodness of Jehovah in the land of the living." Psalms 116:9 says, "I will walk before Jehovah in the land of the living." Psalms 142:5 says, "I cried unto thee, O Jehovah; I said, Thou art my refuge, my portion in the land of the living."

There are some who feel that it would not be possible for God to forsake his own Son, or for Jesus to have to enter Hades, the land of the lost, the land of the dead, the land of the condemned, and be cut off from God—out of the land of the living—to pay for our sins. The only reason for that kind of thinking is because it expects just a little too much of the Most Holy God; for Him to have to suffer such infinite pain and grief himself to take away our sins. With all his power and glory couldn't he have avoided such a horrible fate? But since that is what the Scriptures say, that is what must have happened. All of this just describes the tremendous love of God and the price he and his Son Jesus were willing to pay to become our Savior and maintain their holiness and righteousness in so doing. It also shows the power of the Almighty to be able to accomplish such an achievement.

There are others who find it impossible to believe that the Almighty who left his throne of glory and became the Son of man could have been made to be sin by God himself, and so they change it to "sin-offering" (2 Corinthians 5:21). Paul wrote that when Adam sinned, he made all men sinners (Romans 5:19). However, by the grace of God it was only Jesus who was made to be a sinner or—made to be sin (2 Corinthians 5:21). But by Jesus' cross God made all men righteous—if they will accept him and his sacrifice.

It is best not to go by our feelings and emotions and change the meaning of the Scriptures to suit them. It is best to accept what the Scriptures say word-for-word, and then change our feelings and emotions to accept exactly what the Bible teaches, just as it was written. Maybe anyone who feels that it is asking just a little too much to believe Jesus actually went into Hades to spiritually pay for our sins should also consider that it might be asking just a little too much for the Almighty Jehovah God himself to leave his throne of glory, his inapproachable light (1 Timothy 6:16), and come into this world to be spit on, beaten, blasphemed, mocked, crowned with thorns, nailed to a cross and be lifted up and left to die? (Matthew 27:26–31)—But most all Christians accept that, because that is exactly what he did.

In Acts chapter 2, Jesus was promised by his Father that his body would not be left in the tomb long enough to see corruption, nor would his soul be left in Hades. Therefore, his body had to be in the grave, and his soul had to be in Hades, or those promises would not have meant anything to Jesus. Acts 2:22–33 says:

> Ye men of Israel, hear these words: Jesus of Nazareth, a man approved of God unto you by mighty works and wonders and signs which God did by him in the midst of you, even as ye yourselves know; him, being delivered up by the determinate counsel and foreknowledge of God, ye by the hand of lawless men did crucify and slay: whom God raised up, having loosed the pangs of death: because it was not possible that he should be holden of it. For David saith concerning him, I beheld the Lord always before my face; For he is on my right hand, that I should not be moved: Therefore my heart was glad, and my tongue rejoiced; Moreover my flesh also shall dwell in hope: Because thou wilt not leave my soul unto Hades, neither wilt thou give thy Holy One to see corruption. Thou madest known unto me the ways of life; Thou shalt make me full of gladness with thy countenance. Brethren, I may say unto you freely of the patriarch David, that he both died and was buried, and his tomb is with us unto this day. Being therefore a prophet, and knowing that God had sworn with an oath to him, that of the fruit of his loins he would set one upon his throne; he foreseeing this spake of the resurrection of the Christ, that neither was he left unto Hades, nor did his flesh see corruption. This Jesus did God raise up, whereof we all are witnesses. Being therefore by the right hand of God exalted, and having received of the Father the promise of the

Holy Spirit, he hath poured forth this, which ye see and hear.

Those promises were precious to Jesus because he had given up his equality with God when he became the Son of man (Philippians 2:5–8). That put Jesus into a position where he had no more power over death or Hades than any other man had. When Jesus' body went into the tomb, and his human Spirit went into Hades, his only hope of escaping those dreadful places was by trusting in the faithfulness of his Father, and in his Father's promises. That is also very precious to us because we rely on those same promises! Our resurrection from the grave depends on the same promise that Jesus' Father made to him, and that assures us that the resurrection of all the dead is just as certain for us as it was for Jesus, except we shall never enter Hades because Jesus went there for us.

There is a Scripture in Matthew that states how strongly Jesus believed in his Father's promises. Matthew 16:13–19 says:

> Now when Jesus came into the parts of Caesarea Philippi, he asked his disciples, saying, Who do men say that the Son of man is? And they said, Some say John the Baptist; some, Elijah; and others, Jeremiah, or one of the prophets. He saith unto them, But who say ye that I am? And Simon Peter answered and said, Thou art the Christ, the Son of the living God. And Jesus answered and said unto him, Blessed art thou, Simon Bar-Jonah: for flesh and blood hath not revealed it unto thee, but my Father who is in heaven. And I also say unto thee, that thou art Peter, and upon this rock I will build my church; and the gates of Hades shall not prevail against it. I will give unto thee the keys of the kingdom of heaven: and whatso-

ever thou shalt bind on earth shall be bound in
heaven; and whatsoever thou shalt loose on earth
shall be loosed in heaven.

Jesus said *"the gates"* of Hades could not prevent him from
building his church. He did not say Hades, or hell, or Satan, or
some terrible and powerful evil force imposed a threat to his
plans—only some gates. What is the function of a gate? How
could a gate—any gate—prevail against Jesus building his church?
A gate has only one function: control. A gate controls entrance
or exit to some regulated and secured place. The gates of Hades
only open one way—to allow entrance. Since it was the gates
to Hades that Jesus said could not prevent him from building
his church, that must mean those gates could not prevent him
from entering that dreadful place so he could pay the price God
demanded to save the world from sin and death, nor could they
prevent his exit from that feared place when the time came for
him to leave it. I believe the actual point Jesus made concerning the power of the gates of Hades was—*they could not contain
him*—they had no power to restrain him and thus prevent him
from building his church. At the appointed time of his Father,
Jesus would exit that terrible place and his spirit and soul would
return to his body, and his body would come out of the grave and
live again. That is called the resurrection. Jesus would return to
his disciples and live with them for forty days in the same body
that was crucified, and it was the same body in which he would
build his church, and then ascend into heaven. Jesus disciples
did not believe that was possible, even when they were with him
and could see him and touch him. Luke wrote in his gospel:

And he said unto them, Why are ye troubled? and
wherefore do questionings arise in your heart?
See my hands and my feet, that it is I myself:
handle me, and see; for a spirit hath not flesh and

bones, as ye behold me having. And when he had said this, he showed them his hands and his feet. And while they still disbelieved for joy, and wondered, he said unto them, Have ye here anything to eat? And they gave him a piece of a broiled fish. (Luke 24:38–42)

There is an interesting Scripture in Peter's first epistle that teaches what Jesus did while he was in Hades. First Peter 3:17–22 says:

For it is better, if the will of God should so will, that ye suffer for well-doing than for evil-doing. Because Christ also suffered for sins once, the righteous for the unrighteous, that he might bring us to God; being put to death in the flesh, but made alive in the spirit; in which also he went and preached unto the spirits in prison, that aforetime were disobedient, when the longsuffering of God waited in the days of Noah, while the ark was a preparing, wherein few, that is, eight souls, were saved through water: which also after a true likeness doth now save you, even baptism, not the putting away of the filth of the flesh, but the interrogation of a good conscience toward God, through the resurrection of Jesus Christ; who is on the right hand of God, having gone into heaven; angels and authorities and powers being made subject unto him.

That is a strange passage of Scripture. All we can know about it is what is written right here. We can also reference 1 Peter 4:5–6, just a few verses ahead, and Isaiah chapter 53. Peter said Jesus went in his spirit that had been made alive at the cross to preach to the spirits that were in prison. Jesus was not forced into that place. He was not carried off by the angels and cast into Hades. He went there himself, of his own volition, just as he delivered himself up to be crucified of his own volition (Luke 9:22; 22:37). Jesus entered that appalling place knowing that it was by the promise of his Father he would not be left there. To me it is astonishing that Jesus could leave the cross in his Spirit, find Hades, and then enter that horrible place; *it was a place that he himself had created.* Paul wrote, "...who is the image of the invisible God, the firstborn of all creation; for in him were all things created, in the heavens and upon the earth, things visible and things invisible, whether thrones or dominions or principalities or powers; all things have been created through him, and unto him; and he is before all things, and in him all things consist" (Colossians 1:15-17).

It is also amazing that when the promise of Jesus' Father was fulfilled, it was that promise to his Son that prevented the gates of Hades from holding him in. Jesus went into Hades to pay for our sins. When he left Hades, he left our sins in that dreadful place—a place that is as far away from us as the east is from the west. Psalms103:12 says, "As far as the east is from the west, so far hath he removed our transgressions from us." It might be possible to measure the distance from north to south, the distance between the poles, but not from east to west, for that measurement is not imaginable.

But there are questions: Why would Jesus preach to spirits in prison, or Hades, when there was no hope of escape from that horrible place? Why did he preach only to those who had died in the 120-year period of the flood while Noah was building the ark? How could the Spirit of Jesus be *"made alive"*? It was Jesus' human Spirit that died when he was forsaken by God (Isaiah 53:12), and so it was his human Spirit that was made alive. A living spirit cannot be made alive; it is alive. Only a dead spirit can be made alive. There are no answers to those questions anywhere in the Bible, except in Isaiah chapter 53, and 1 Peter 4:3-6.

According to what was written in *The Genesis Flood*; by John Whitcomb and Henry Morris, the most conservative estimate for the population of the world 1656 after the creation (about 2,400 B.C.—the year of the flood) was 1.03 billion. That is about what the population of the earth was in the year 1800 A.D. The population of the world when God destroyed it with the flood could have been as great as it is today, we just do not know. That's because, before the flood, people lived for some nine-hundred years, and longer (Genesis 5:25-27). Maybe when God saw so many perish in such a violent manner, he had a plan to offer them another chance—a chance to leave that dreadful place called Hades—if they would only listen to his Son who was right there with them and teaching them. If only they would believe the message that Jesus preached to them, the gospel, they could be forgiven of their sins, and they could leave that horrible place with Jesus when he left it. The question is: Does the cross of Jesus have the power of God that is so great, and so mighty, that it could have extended into Hades and accomplished such a feat at the time when Jesus went there? Did Jesus and his cross have the authority of God's grace and mercy to offer forgiveness to those who had perished in the flood? Could it have been possible that if they would just believe what Jesus taught them (that He truly was the Son of God who had died on a cross for all sin, including their sins) that they could escape Hades and leave it with Jesus when he left? That did happen, but it happened only once, because Jesus was crucified only once, and therefore he went to preach to the spirits in prison only once—But he certainly did do it once, the Bible says so. It is sad that we don't know if anyone responded to Jesus' teaching, or what resulted from his preaching the gospel to the spirits in prison. Did anyone believe him and leave with him? We just do not know. Only God knows.

My view is: He might just have completely emptied that place of any inhabitants.

It was the Spirit of Christ, his human Spirit that went and preached to the spirits in prison (Hades)—not the Holy Spirit. The Holy Spirit cannot be made alive. The Holy Spirit is always alive and always vibrant with life. He is the giver of life.

Immediately after Jesus' death his body was entombed. At that moment Jesus' human Spirit also died and was forsaken by God (Isaiah 53:11–12; Matthew 27:46). That is when Jesus' spirit was "cut off out of the land of the living" (Isaiah 53:8); he poured out his soul unto death (Isaiah 53:12); and his soul was made an offering for sin. All sacrifices that are offered to God as sin-offerings must die to make that sacrifice (Isaiah 53:10). Even Jesus had to die on the cross for his sin-offering to be valid. That is when God saw the travail of his soul and was satisfied (Isaiah 53:11). (That is the cup Jesus prayed to God he would not have to drink, Matthew 26:38-44, and all of this is something that is infinitely deep and so far past human reasoning that it can never be fully understood; but it can be believed, appreciated—and accepted as true—by believing it in faith.)

What we are viewing is what it cost God to forgive us of our sins, and what Jesus was willing to pay to correct all the problems, devastation, and pain that sin had caused—and to restore the creation back to God in all its original beauty, glory, and perfection, and "*much more.*" But Jesus had never sinned, and so the death he suffered—physically and spiritually—was for Adam's sin and for our sins. For men to be perfectly set free from sin and death full payment had to be made to satisfy both spiritual death and physical death (Romans 3:23–26). Jesus paid that price in full when he took all the punishment that was due to fall upon sinners, upon himself. We truly have been set free from sin, death, and law, by Jesus and his cross.

It is difficult to understand when Jesus' Spirit was "made alive." Was it before he went into Hades or when he left Hades?

If his Spirit was made alive before he went into Hades, he would be the only living spirit in the realm of the dead. That would have made a tremendous impression upon those in Hades to whom Jesus preached the gospel. Therefore, when the gospel was being preached over the entire face of the earth by the Christians (Colossians 1:5–6) offering the forgiveness of sin and eternal life to all men everywhere, it was also being preached in Hades by Jesus himself—offering the forgiveness of sin and eternal life to an elect group of people: to those who had perished in the flood. When Jesus was in Hades peaching the Word, God's grace was extended into the realm of the dead (1 Peter 4:5-6). Why it was extended only to those who had died within a 120-year period—the time period of the flood while Noah was building the ark—is a question only God can answer. However, because of the long lives that men lived, most of the people who died from the time of Adam to the time of Noah perished in the flood. Adam lived 930 years after creation. The flood took place 1656 after the creation, which at that time was only about two generations among men from Adam until the flood.

It was the Spirit of God's Son, Jesus, not Noah who preached the gospel to those who were in prison. Noah was a preacher of righteousness (2 Peter 2:5), but here Scripture says it was the Spirit of Christ who preached to those who were in prison—because they had been disobedient in the days of Noah. There is another statement in Peter's first epistle about the gospel being preached to those who were in prison, or to the dead. It is in the same context and almost in the same sentence as the previous Scripture about Jesus preaching to the spirits in prison. Therefore, it must be speaking of the same thing. First Peter 4:3–6 says:

> For the time past may suffice to have wrought
> the desire of the Gentiles, and to have walked in
> lasciviousness, lusts, winebibbings, revellings,

carousings, and abominable idolatries: wherein they think strange that ye run not with them into the same excess of riot, speaking evil of you: who shall give account to him that is ready to judge the living and the dead. For unto this end was the gospel preached even to the dead, that they might be judged indeed according to men in the flesh, but live according to God in the spirit.

The point Peter made is: all men shall stand before God to be judged (Romans 14:11-12; 2 Corinthians 5:10). If a person is alive at the end of time when Jesus comes to judge the world, he shall be judged in his flesh—but if a person dies before Jesus comes, he shall still be judged, for dying does not allow a person to escape the judgment (Hebrews 9:27). The message of Peter is because God is going to judge the living and the dead, the gospel was preached even to the dead, so that those who heard it could escape the punishment they deserved for all the sins they had committed. That punishment was death! —but it was a death they had already experienced. But through the preaching of Jesus and his gospel they could live again and have eternal life. All of that was accomplished because of the infinite magnitude of God's love, mercy, and grace—caring even for those who had already perished and were being punished for their sins. That is the reason God saw fit to allow the gospel to be preached *even to the dead*— "even" meaning that it was a rare and exceptional case—it would happen only once. Paul and the other apostles had preached the gospel to the whole world of the living in some thirty or forty years after Jesus had died (Colossians 1:3–6). But someone else preached the gospel *even to the dead.*

There are questions that must be asked to find the answers to those difficult scriptures. First, who preached the gospel *"even to the dead?"* Who were the dead to whom the gospel was preached? Why was the gospel preached even to the dead?

When and where was the gospel preached to the dead? The answer to the first question is: it was Jesus who preached the gospel to the dead, and that happened when he went in his Spirit and preached to the spirits in prison (1 Peter 3:18–19). The dead to whom the gospel was preached were the spirits of men who were in prison because aforetime, long before the cross, in the days of Noah, they had been disobedient, and they had perished in the flood for their transgression. But why would the gospel be preached to spirits in prison—spirits who were dead—when from that dreaded place called Hades there was no hope and no escape? The answer to that question is found in the verse itself. The gospel was preached to the dead so they could be judged indeed according to men living in the flesh, as if they were still alive, breathing, and living in their flesh-and-blood bodies—and they had never died. For the time a person is alive, and they can hear the gospel, they can obey it and have their sins forgiven and enter into eternal life. The thief who died with Jesus on the cross and was forgiven of his sins just moments before he died proves that. But after a person dies it is too late. But here, the dead to whom the gospel was preached were being offered the same blessing that is always offered to those who are still living. They were offered the opportunity of hearing the gospel, and thus offered the opportunity to obey it and have their sins forgiven, just as if they were still living in their physical bodies. If this scripture does not say that, just exactly what does it say?

Another reason the gospel was preached even to the dead was so they could live again according to God in the spirit. The spirits of the men to whom the gospel was preached were dead. They were separated from God because of sin, and they were in prison. Therefore, they were dead because of sin. However, Jesus was offering them the opportunity to hear and believe the gospel just as if they were still living in their bodies, and by hearing and believing the gospel their sins could be forgiven, their spirits could be made alive again, and they could live with God in their renewed spirits forever. This just demonstrates how powerful, how amazing, and how wonderful the love, the grace, and the mercy of God are. It also demonstrates how great the love of God is for all his children, the living, and the dead. God is the creator of life, the giver of life, and the great lover of life, and that is why he created so much of it, and that is why Jesus died to save it.

If a person feels it was just not possible for the gospel to have been preached to spirits in Hades because—it just seems impossible and unreasonable—and the Scriptures that say he did do that must mean something else rather than what they say. In that case, they should consider the grace, the mercy, and the love of God that every living person has been given by the blood of God's Son, Jesus. Isn't it possible that God still loves the dead just as dearly as he loves people who are living, even though they were gross, evil, wicked, and immoral sinners? Paul wrote in the Roman letter:

> While we were yet weak, in due season Christ died for the ungodly. For scarcely for a righteous man will one die: for peradventure for the good man some one would even dare to die. But God commendeth his own love toward us, in that, while we were yet sinners, Christ died for us. Much more then, being now justified by his blood, shall we be saved from the wrath of God through him. For if, while we were enemies, we were reconciled to God through the death of his Son, much more, being reconciled, shall we be saved by his life. (Romans 5:6–10)

If God loved evil, immoral, wicked sinners so much when they were still living in the worst of their sins that he sent his Son to die for them—because he wanted to forgive them—isn't it possible that God has the same love for the dead, and he wanted to give them another chance at life—if they would only believe in his Son during that one and only occasion when he was right there with them? If a person refuses to believe such was possible, it is not because of what the scriptures say, or because they are difficult to understand. The scriptures are very clear on this point. Also, if the above seems to be unreasonable, then what about the thief who died on the cross at the same time Jesus died? One moment he was chastising and mocking Jesus along with all of those who were witnessing the suffering that he was enduring (Matthew 27:39–44). He even admitted that he was the worst of criminals and deserved the punishment he was receiving (Luke 23:39–43). But in the last few moments of his life he repented, and he looked over to Jesus and said he was so sorry, "please remember me when you come into your kingdom." Jesus forgave him, and is that love and forgiveness any greater or lesser than what God offered the spirits who were in prison?

CONCLUSION

THE LAW OF MOSES was given to let men know what God required of them, and to guide them in the way they should live. It was also given to establish the forgiveness of sin so that when a person broke the law and sinned, they had a way to be pardoned and live. Romans 5:20–21 says, "And the law came in besides, that the trespass might abound; but where sin abounded, grace did abound more exceedingly: that, as sin reigned in death, even so might grace reign through righteousness unto eternal life through Jesus Christ our Lord." Paul wrote:

> Now this I say: A covenant confirmed beforehand by God, the law, which came four hundred and thirty years after, doth not disannul, so as to make the promise of none effect. For if the inheritance is of the law, it is no more of promise: but God hath granted it to Abraham by promise. What then is the law? It was added because of transgressions, till the seed should come to whom the promise hath been made; and it was ordained through angels by the hand of a mediator. Now a

mediator is not a mediator of one; but God is one. Is the law then against the promises of God? God forbid: for if there had been a law given which could make alive, verily righteousness would have been of the law. But the scriptures shut up all things under sin, that the promise by faith in Jesus Christ might be given to them that believe. But before faith came, we were kept in ward under the law, shut up unto the faith which should afterwards be revealed. So that the law is become our tutor to bring us unto Christ, that we might be justified by faith. But now that faith is come, we are no longer under a tutor. (Galatians 3:17–25)

The law was added because of transgressions so the trespass might abound. The trespass was not greater just because the law came into effect; it was greater because it had a standard by which it could be exposed and measured as to just how serious it was. If there had been a law that said, "Thou shall not kill" when Cain slew his brother Abel, and the penalty for committing such a crime demanded the murderer be stoned to death, Cain would have understood what a horrible crime he had committed. But when a person sinned and there was no established penalty available to reflect the seriousness of their trespass, it would be difficult to know how to administer justice. But when a person sinned, and there was a law that plainly called attention to the trespass and specified the punishment that was to be administered for every transgression, that would truly establish how serious the sin was, or make the trespass *abound*. But when sin abounded, grace abounded even more. God's grace is greater than all sin. The power of God to forgive is much greater than the power sin has to condemn.

With the coming of knowledge of good and evil, and the coming of the law, the standard of right and wrong was perfectly established. When people sinned under law, they sinned against God exactly as Adam had trespassed against the Almighty—that is, they sinned by breaking God's law—(and Adam had only one law he could break). When Adam sinned, the law he was under declared exactly what the punishment was for breaking that law. It did not offer forgiveness—but that was something the Almighty did anyway because of his love, his mercy, and his grace. With the establishment of the law and the forgiveness of sin through animal sacrifices, the reign of God's grace began, and the reign of death ended. The reign of death could not coexist with the reign of grace; and the reign of grace could not exist without destroying the reign of death, and so that is exactly what Jesus did with his cross.

El Fin

www.ingramcontent.com/pod-product-compliance
Lightning Source LLC
LaVergne TN
LVHW011227080426
835509LV00005B/361